A Complete Introduction to the World of Web Design: A Visual Approach

Haider Syed

I am indebted to my family whose support played a pivotal role in enabling me to successfully write this book.

I dedicate this book to my family: Rakshinda Waheed (my mother), Syed Waheed Ahmed (my father), Sana Syed (my sister) and Wasif Syed (my brother).

- Haider Syed
2004

The first thing that comes to a person's mind is "What is HTML? Who should learn HTML? Why should I learn it? And how long will it take to learn HTML?" Let us start off by answering all of these questions.

HTML is the abbreviation for *H*yper*T*ext *M*arkup *L*anguage. Anyone who wants to make a professional or even basic website should learn HTML. HTML is very easy to learn and get the hang of and is quite useful to know. If you are really determined, you can learn it within just a week.

Almost every tutorial you will come across may appear boring in the beginning; however as you progress, it will become more enjoyable. You must not give up. Before you start, you must understand that this is a technical book. The chapters are designed to be worked through in succession and skipping ahead may leave you confused if you are a novice. Feel free to jump around if you already have had experience in web designing and with using HTML in particular and feel that you are well acquainted with some of the material covered in the early chapters.

Intended Audience:

This book can benefit a wide range of audiences but is primarily intended to introduce a complete beginner to the world of web design and HTML. It is aimed at anyone who would like to learn HTML to make web pages on a casual basis or a professional who would like to make high quality, aesthetically pleasing websites. The book is designed so that it can cater to the needs of both a novice as well as a more informed HTML user who would like a good reference guide. Furthermore, this book's intended audience also encompasses educators, teachers and instructors at schools, universities and other technical institutions who are looking for a book on web design to complement their course material or to serve as a main course book. A student interested in web design will also find it to be a useful addition to his reference library.

Required Skills:

In order to fully understand this tutorial, it is recommended that you know how to use a computer. In general, this means, being able to perform simple tasks such as copying and pasting and following simple instructions such as saving your work and opening programs, etc. I have tried to make this book very **user friendly** (easy to follow even for novices) so even if your computer skills are a bit rusty, you should still be able to understand what you are supposed to do.

Before you start:

It is worth noting that the number of tasks that one can accomplish with HTML is limited. You cannot build flashy websites with dancing cartoons using HTML alone. Basically, it is not designed for layout but more for content. However, it is a fundamental language for website designing and by far one of the easiest languages you can learn. You can make high-quality websites but there is a lot of work involved. Using HTML, you can insert pictures, music, writing, backgrounds, email links, buttons, forms, etc to your web pages. It is not a good idea for the novice user to learn some of the advanced languages before he/she has learnt HTML adequately as that can prove to be quite difficult and may leave him/her confused. It should also be known that most of the advanced languages require a good background in HTML. With this in mind, you should look at HTML as your first step into the world of webpage designing.

At the time when the book was sent to the publisher to be printed, the intention was to publish the entire book in color. However due to certain logistics that arose in the last minute, the book interior had to be published in black and white. Thus as it is important to be able to see color in the screenshots and figures in certain sections of the book, for the reader's convenience, I have uploaded those pages online on the following website:

http://www.wbook.info

Readers can go to the above website and download the relevant sections in color.

I would appreciate feedback from readers regarding this book. If you have any comments, suggestions or questions about this book, please feel free to contact me at hsyed1@gmail.com. Also, I would appreciate it if you would contact me should you find any typographical errors.

Thank you. I hope you enjoy the journey through the wonderful world of web design!

Good luck.

Haider Syed

CONVENTIONS USED IN THIS BOOK

In the HTML section of this book, you will see boxes entitled HTML TIPS. For example:

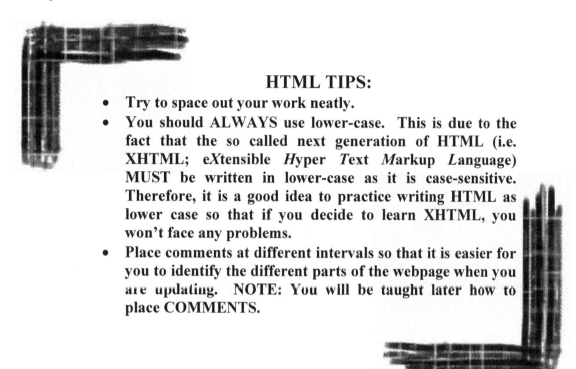

HTML TIPS:

- **Try to space out your work neatly.**
- **You should ALWAYS use lower-case. This is due to the fact that the so called next generation of HTML (i.e. XHTML; eXtensible Hyper Text Markup Language) MUST be written in lower-case as it is case-sensitive. Therefore, it is a good idea to practice writing HTML as lower case so that if you decide to learn XHTML, you won't face any problems.**
- **Place comments at different intervals so that it is easier for you to identify the different parts of the webpage when you are updating. NOTE: You will be taught later how to place COMMENTS.**

These boxes contain useful and important tips which you should read as they provide valuable information.

You will also come across short notes. For example:

NOTE: Text enclosed by the <title> tag means text that you write between the starting and ending <title> tag.

These highlight important points that you should be aware of.

HTML code will usually be written in UPPERCASE except the attribute values. This will help you differentiate between the text that will be displayed on the webpage and the actual background coding which visitors to your website won't see. The exception to this is when the coding is quite long in which case uppercase has been avoided. For example, most web pages in Chapter 5 have been written as a mixture of lower case and upper case since lower case tends to be easier on the eyes.

Most of the screenshots in this book have been cropped. That means that they have basically been cut down to only display the requisite portion of the screen.

SECTION A:
LEARNING HTML

HTML does not require any special software. All you need is a text-editor to make the files and a web browser to view the files. I recommend that you use "Notepad" as the text-editor. Notepad should already be installed on your computer. Don't use programs such as Microsoft Word for typing in the HTML code as it can give rise to certain complications.

FOR EXTREME BEGINNERS

(Skip this section if you know how to make a folder and open Notepad.)

MAKE A FOLDER: It is a good idea to make a folder so that all the web pages you create are in one place. In order to make a folder in My Documents, follow the following steps:

1. Double-click on the 'My Documents' icon on the desktop

The My Documents folder should now open and you will see the screen shown in Figure 1.1.

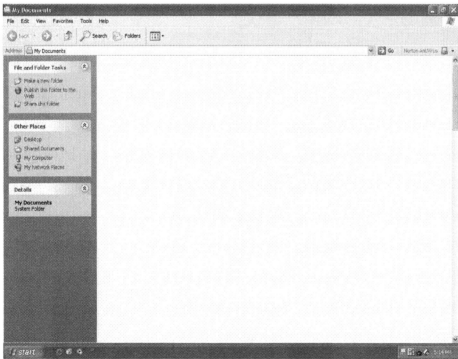

FIGURE 1.1: Screen shot of My Documents folder

2. Right-click on the white area and select New (Figure 1.2)

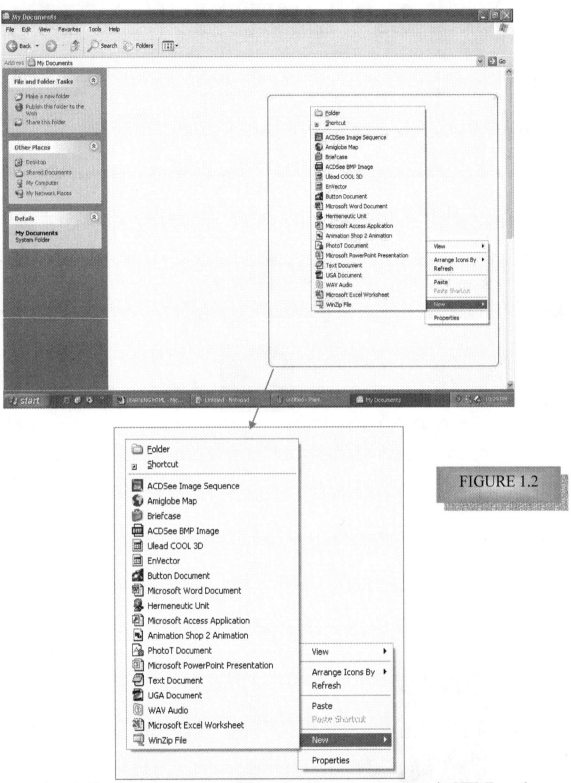

FIGURE 1.2

3. Select Folder from the menu. A folder should now appear; type in HTML as the name for the folder and press enter.

OPENING NOTEPAD: When you turn on the computer your operating system loads up. An example of a popular operating system is Windows XP. What appears after loading is your desktop. Figure 1.3 shows an example of a typical desktop for Windows XP. In order to open Notepad, click on the "start" button on the bottom, left corner.

Click
Here

FIGURE 1.3: A typical windows XP Desktop

10

Figure 1.4 illustrates the menu that you should see after clicking the start button.

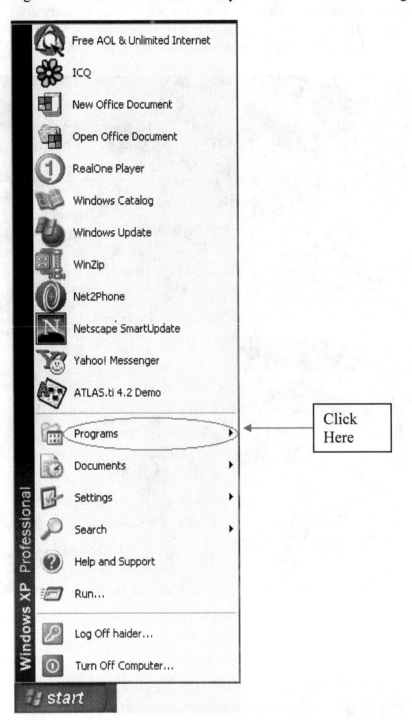

FIGURE 1.4: The Start menu

From the start menu select "Programs" (Figure 1.5).

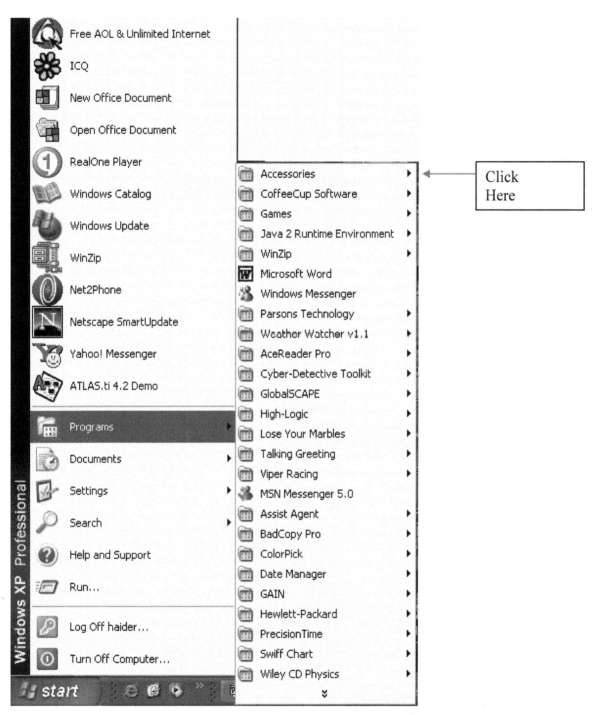

FIGURE 1.5: You should see the following menu pop-up after clicking on Programs.

Choose Accessories from the menu that now appears (Figure 1.6) and click on Notepad.

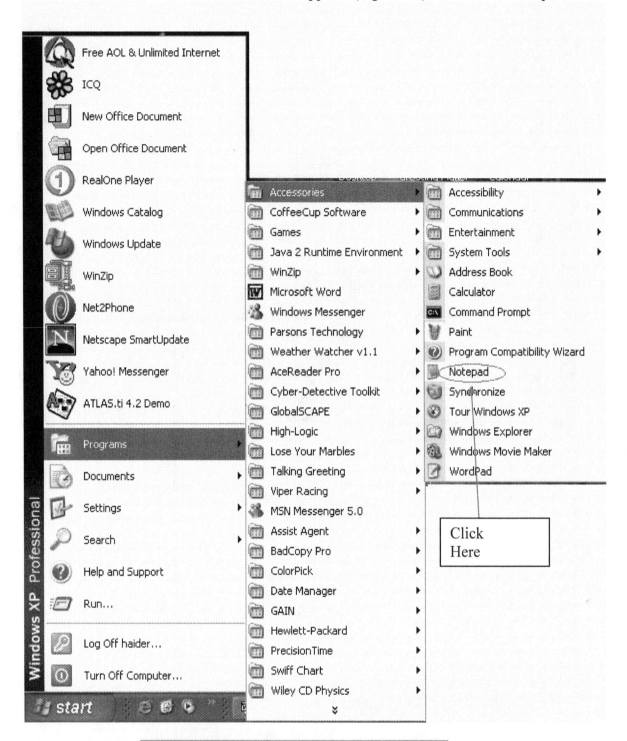

FIGURE 1.6: Click once on Accessories

Notepad will now open (Figure 1.7).

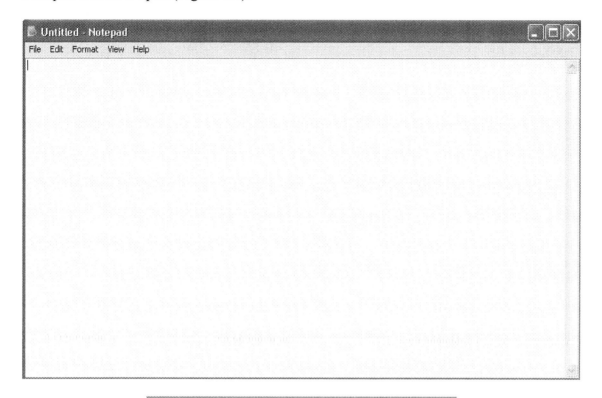

FIGURE 1.7: Screenshot of Notepad

If you skipped the last section, make sure you make a folder called "HTML" in My Documents. Save all the web pages you create in this folder.

Note: It does not make a difference where you create the folder (on your desktop, My Documents, hard disk, etc.) but I do recommend that you create one so that all your work is saved in one place.

The syntax for HTML coding is very similar to English so the basics are easy to remember.

It is worth remembering that computer languages whose instructions are very similar to English are called **High-level languages**. HTML is just one example of a high-level language. The other class of computer languages is called **Low-level languages**. These languages have instructions which are similar to the machine code of the computer. Each type of language has its own advantages and disadvantages. With these in mind the programmers decide which one would be best tailored for their specific projects.

When we write an HTML instruction, it is called a TAG.

Computers don't understand English, so in order to interact with the computer, you must learn computer languages. Computers can only process binary digits (zeros and ones). HTML is a computer language that is used specifically for web designing.

14

HTML code is written in Notepad. When the file is saved, **.html** is written at the end of the file name which results in the file being saved as a webpage file and not as a text file (the letters that appear in a filename after the period are known as the "file extension"). Every html file must begin with the command **<HTML>**. Note that the "less than" and "greater than" signs (< and >) are used with every **tag**. A **tag** is the name given to an HTML instruction, for example: <B>.

When a browser comes across a **tag**, it knows that it is an HTML instruction and the text between the < and > sign will *not* be displayed on the webpage.

Don't worry about remembering all this theory; it will be covered in more depth at a later stage. For now, let's start off with our first webpage.

Open Notepad and type in the following lines of code.

```
<HTML>
This is my first webpage.
</HTML>
```

To save the file, follow the steps given below:

1. Click on File. Then choose Save As… from the pull-down menu (Figure 1.8)

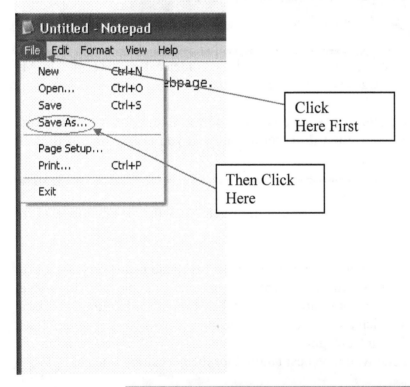

FIGURE 1.8: Saving an html file, Step 1

2. You should now see the Save As dialog box (Figure 1.9).

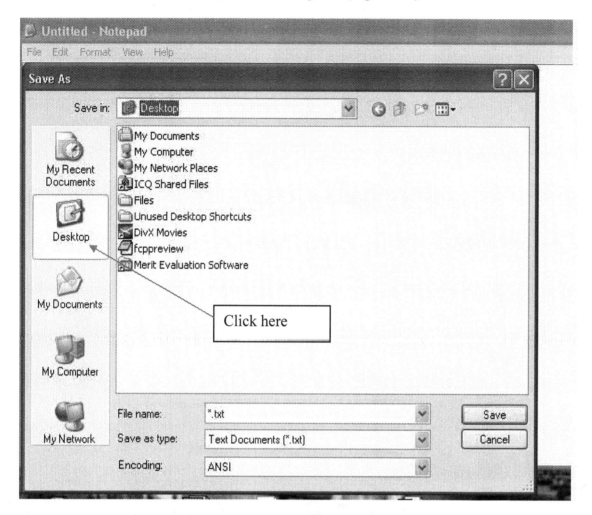

Click here

Click on My Documents from the side (Figure 1.9) and choose the folder that you created called **HTML**. In the "File name" row, delete any text that is already present and type in "first.html"

Make sure that you type in **.html** after the file name. As stated earlier, this is called the extension of the file and is crucial. Without it, the browser will not recognize the file as a webpage.

You have just created and saved your first webpage. The next step now is to view the webpage in the browser. My personal preference is Internet Explorer but Netscape will do just fine too.

1. Open Internet Explorer and click on File and select Open... (Figure 1.10).

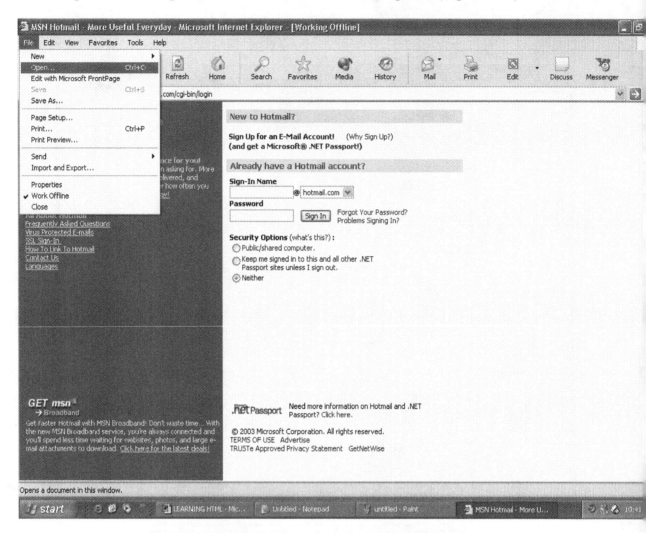

FIGURE 1.10: Opening your webpage in a browser, Step 1

2. Click on Browse from the Open dialog box that appears. You should now see the screen shown in Figure 1.11

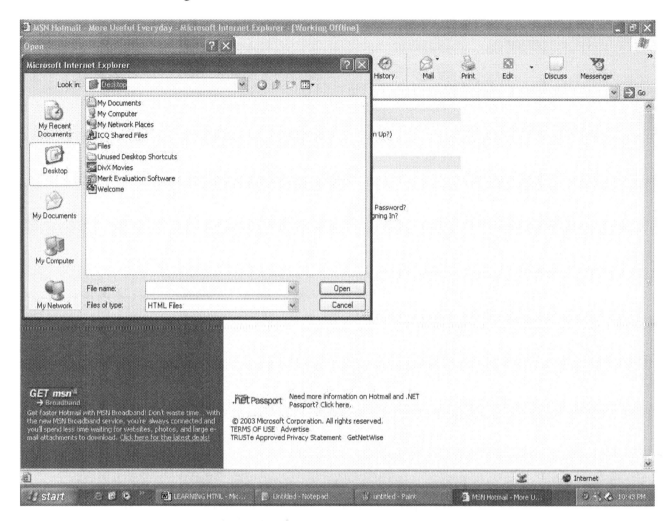

FIGURE 1.11: Opening your webpage in a browser, Step 2

Select My Documents from the left side. Click on the folder you created called HTML and then double-click on "first.html". Click Open and your webpage should now open (Figure 1.11).

FIGURE 1.11: The webpage as viewed in a browser

18

Now for a bit of theory, HTML is not case-sensitive which means that it can either be written in capital letters or small letters (i.e. upper or lower case). For example: You can use

<HTML> **OR** <html>

The first word that follows the '**<**' is called an element: Example: <FONT>
Elements can have different properties or values which are referred to as attributes:
Example <font color = "yellow">
'color' is the **attribute** in this example and 'yellow' is the **value** of the attribute.

Let's have another look at the coding for the webpage which we just created. The coding is called source code in computer terms.

```
<HTML>
This is my first html document.
</HTML>
```

Notice that there are two HTML tags in this document and the second one has a slash (/) following the < sign. This is called a closing tag and it basically represents the end of the first tag. So, in this case the first tag (<html>) starts the html document and the second one (</html>) tells the browser that the html document has ended. Anything in between is displayed as text (in this case). This is the most fundamental layout of an html document. Remember, almost every tag has a **closing/ending tag**. The only difference between an 'end tag' and the 'starting tag' is that an end tag has a "right slash (/)" after the < sign

Another example of a starting tag and an end tag is as follows:

Opening tag: <HEAD>
Closing tag: </HEAD>

So far we have just learned how to start and end an HTML document. We will now learn how to make a more organized HTML document.

Type in the following information into Notepad and save the file as "title.html":

```
<HTML>
<HEAD>
<TITLE>
My first title.
</TITLE>
</HEAD>
</HTML>
```

Make sure that you type in **.html** at the end of file name because otherwise the browser will not recognize your file as a webpage.

View your webpage in a browser and read the definitions below.

<HTML> This tag tells the browser that the coding that follows is written in HTML.

<HEAD> The information that follows this tag is related with the head (top) portion of the browser and will not be displayed in the actual body of the webpage.

<TITLE> Text enclosed between the title tag (i.e. what you type between the start and end title tag) will be displayed in the reverse bar (blue bar at the top of the document; refer to Figure 1.12).

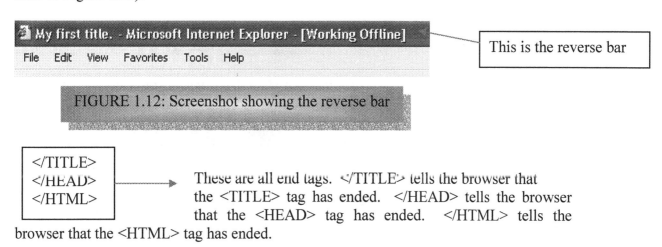

FIGURE 1.12: Screenshot showing the reverse bar

</TITLE>
</HEAD>
</HTML>

These are all end tags. </TITLE> tells the browser that the <TITLE> tag has ended. </HEAD> tells the browser that the <HEAD> tag has ended. </HTML> tells the browser that the <HTML> tag has ended.

If you typed the code properly, your screen should look like the screenshot in Figure 1.13.

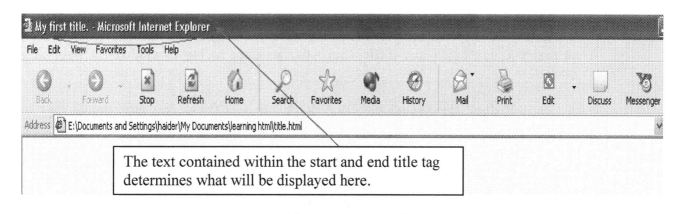

The text contained within the start and end title tag determines what will be displayed here.

FIGURE 1.13: The effect of the title tag

So far we have covered how to change the text in the reverse bar; in order to add text to the body of the webpage we use the <BODY> tag.

NOTE: Text enclosed by the <title> tag refers to the text that you write between the starting and ending <title> tag.

Type in the following into Notepad and save the file as "body.html":

```
<HTML>
<HEAD>
<TITLE>The body tag</TITLE>
</HEAD>
<BODY>
This is the body of the document.  Text that is inside it is displayed in the body of the
document.  If you were to write text between the <HEAD> tag, it would not be displayed
unless it is enclosed by the title tag in which case it would appear in the reverse bar.
</BODY>
</HTML>
```

Figure 1.14 shows a screenshot of what you should see when you view the page in a browser.

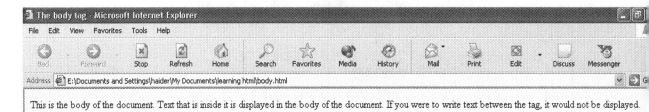

FIGURE 1.14: Adding text to the body of the web page

NOTE: All the tags can be written on one line but it is better that you space your work out and keep one tag per line as a general rule. This will make it easier to read so that you don't face any difficulties when you are trying to modify the page at a later date.

If you still don't understand the tags, don't worry. These are very simple tags to remember. Practice will help you to better understand and remember the tags.

EXERCISE 1:

1) Make a webpage with the title "I love html".
2) Make a webpage which contains the following lines.
   HTML is not case-sensitive. HTML is very easy to learn. The Head tag is followed by the title tag which tells the browser what to display on top.
3) Make a webpage which has the title HTML and in the body contains the following text.
   It is important to understand all the tags covered so far because these are the extreme basics and if I don't understand them, then it is not possible to continue. If you are still a bit unsure, don't worry as it is normal to take some time to actually absorb all this. Now the next thing you should do is practice some more until you get a hang of all the tags. It is crucial that you practice as we go otherwise you will forget everything. It is not possible to learn HTML without practicing it. Remember, practice makes perfect.

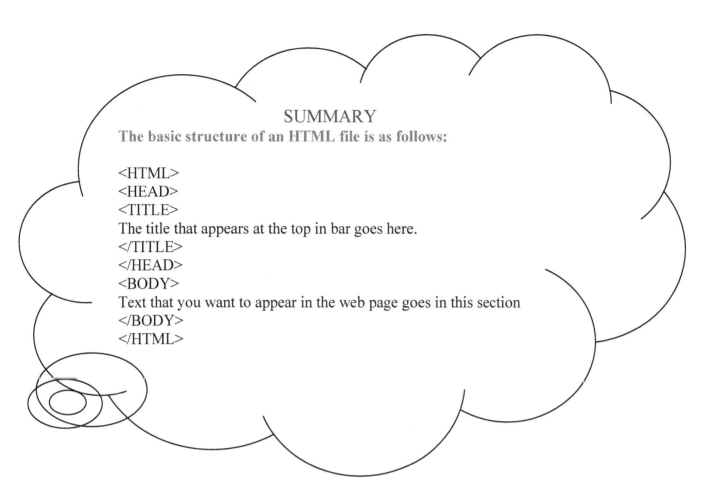

SUMMARY
The basic structure of an HTML file is as follows:

<HTML>
<HEAD>
<TITLE>
The title that appears at the top in bar goes here.
</TITLE>
</HEAD>
<BODY>
Text that you want to appear in the web page goes in this section
</BODY>
</HTML>

So far, we have focused on the extreme basics of HTML. You have learned that:

<HTML> starts off the document.
</HTML> ends the document.

In between these two tags you can have <HEAD> tag and a <TITLE> tag which specifies what is to be displayed at the top of the page. If you only type in text within the <HEAD> tag pairs (as in, underneath this tag) and don't use the <TITLE> tag, the text will not appear on the page and will just be ignored.

In this section you will learn how to:

- Change the font, color and size of text
- Make paragraphs
- Add spaces
- Type text on a new line
- Use typewriter text
- Use preformatted text
- Make text bold, italicizing text and underlining it.

Text Font

Type in the following html code and save it as "fonttype.html"

```
<HTML>
<HEAD>
<TITLE>
Changing the font type
</TITLE>
</HEAD>
<BODY>
<FONT FACE = "Arial">You can also change the font color of text by using the font tag as discussed next. This text should be displayed in Arial. </FONT>
</BODY>
</HTML>
```

When you view the web page in a browser, you should see the screen shown in Figure 2.0

FIGURE 2.0: Specifying a font

The Font tag is <FONT>. **FACE** is the attribute and **Arial** is the value of the attribute in this case. Replace the word **Arial** with the name of the font you require. Be sure to end the tag by typing </FONT>. The text you want to be displayed in Arial font should be written between <FONT FACE = "Arial"> & </FONT>.

<FONT FACE = "Arial">.............</FONT>

Sometimes users will not have the font that you have specified installed on their computer so it is a good idea to specify alternative fonts.

To specify alternative fonts, just type in the alternative fonts you would like to use separated by commas as shown below:

<FONT FACE = "Arial, Black Chancery, Times New Roman"> this text will be displayed as Arial. However, if that font is not installed on your system, it will appear as Black Chancery and finally if that isn't installed on your system, it will appear as Times New Roman. </FONT>

Font Color

The font color of the text can also be changed. In order to do this, the font tag is used once again.

Type in the following code and save the file as "fontcol.html"

```
<HTML>
<HEAD>
<TITLE>
Changing the font color
</TITLE>
</HEAD>
<BODY>
<FONT COLOR="blue">This text should be blue</FONT>
</BODY>
</HTML>
```

When you open the file in your browser, you should see the screen shown in Figure 2.1

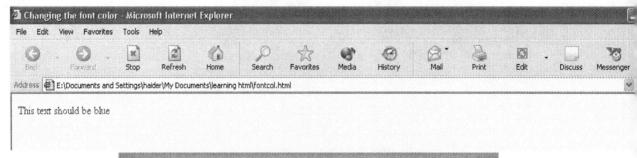

FIGURE 2.1: Changing the font color of text

Please note that as stated in the introduction, at the time when the book was sent to the publisher, the intention was to publish the entire book in color. However due to certain logistics that arose in the last minute, the book interior had to be published in black and white. Thus for the reader's convenience, I have uploaded the pages where color is important on the following website:

http://www.wbook.info

Readers can go to the above website and download the relevant sections in color.

Displaying the different shades of color

To display the different shades, we use **hexadecimals**. It works like this. Instead of you typing in a color name, you type in 6 digits. Every two digits represent one color (**R**ed, **G**reen and **B**lue). **RGB**. The first two digits tell the browser the intensity of red color, the next two digits tell the browser the intensity of green and the fifth and sixth digits specify the intensity of blue to use (i.e. **RRGGBB**). You specify the colors using a range between 0-9 and A-F (for each color). Using this method allows you to create thousands and thousands of different shade colors. Below is an example:

<BODY BGCOLOR = "#000000">

Note: You must always place a number sign (i.e. #) before you write the RGB values (for example: #399933) although it should still work without it. (Note # also goes by the name "hash sign" or "pound sign").

Fortunately, you don't have to experiment for hours to find the right color; there are **many** web sites on the Internet which tell you the different color combinations.

Two of these websites are given below:

http://www.e-pixs.com/colors2.html
http://www.netkontoret.dk/htmlhexcolors.htm

There is also a program which can be downloaded at www.colormix.com. The program gives you the Hexadecimal value for the color which you select on the screen.

Hexadecimals will be discussed in more detail in the next chapter when we deal with changing the background color of web pages.

Font Size

You can change the font size of text using the Font tag. Type in the following code and save it as "fontsize.html":

```
<HTML>
<HEAD>
<TITLE>
How to change font size
</TITLE>
</HEAD>
<BODY>
<FONT SIZE="10">This text should be quite big.  The numbering system with web
pages is not the same as with Microsoft word etc...</FONT>
</BODY>
</HTML>
```

Open the file in a browser and you should now see the screen shown in Figure 2.2.

FIGURE 2.2: Changing the font size of text

If you want to specify a header and don't want to add a font tag, a shorter version is also available as illustrated below.

Type in the following code and save the file as "headers.html"

```
<HTML>
<HEAD>
<TITLE>
Easier way of adding headings
</TITLE>
</HEAD>
<BODY>
<H1> As you can see, this text is quite large and you don't have to do a lot of typing to
achieve this goal either. </H1>
</BODY>
</HTML>
```

Figure 2.3 shows what you should see when you view the file in a browser.

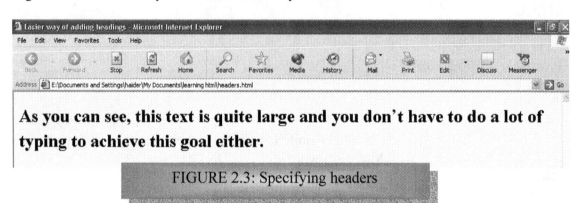

FIGURE 2.3: Specifying headers

You can also use H2, H3, H4, H5 and H6. The greater the number becomes the smaller the text displayed will be. H6 is the smallest text. H1 is the largest possible text size using this tag. Beyond H6, the numbers will have no effect on the text.

Making paragraphs

This is a very short and simple tag

Type in the following HTML code and save the file under the name "para.html"

```
<HTML>
<HEAD><TITLE>Making paragraphs.</TITLE></HEAD>
<BODY>
<P>This is the first paragraph. </P>
<P>This is the second paragraph. </P>
</BODY>
</HTML>
```

The screenshot shown in Figure 2.4 shows what you should see when you view the code in a browser.

FIGURE 2.4: Making paragraphs

You may have noticed that when you added a paragraph by entering text on the next line in the source code, the text was still all displayed as one line in the webpage. This is the way it is in HTML. In order to add new paragraphs you need to use the <p> tag.

Paragraph Alignment

You can align your paragraphs using the <P> tag. This is done by adding the align attribute to the tag.

To align left, you type

<P ALIGN = left> The paragraph that you want aligned left goes here </P>

Similarly, to align to the center of the page, you type

<P ALIGN = center> The paragraph that should be aligned to the center of the page goes here </P>

To align the paragraph to the right of the page, you have to type the following

<P ALIGN = right> The paragraph that should be aligned to the right of the page goes here </P>

As you can see, this is a very simple concept, just to clarify it and to continue the trend in this book, let's look at an example.

Type in the following code into a Notepad file and save it as "para alignment.html":

```
<HTML>
<HEAD>
<TITLE>
Aligning Paragraphs
</TITLE>
</HEAD>
<BODY>
<P ALIGN =left> This paragraph should be aligned to the left of the page </P>

<P ALIGN =center> This paragraph should be aligned to the center of the page </P>
```

<P ALIGN =right> This paragraph should be aligned to the right of the page </P>

<P> The alignment for this paragraph has not been set, so the browser will use the default alignment. </P>
</BODY>
</HTML>

The fourth paragraph in the above coding does not have an align command associated with it; it is therefore aligned to the default position, which is left aligned.

Figure 2.5 shows what the code will appear as in the browser

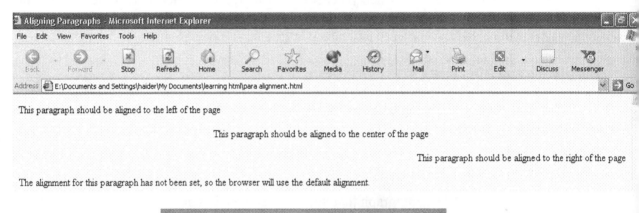

FIGURE 2.5: Paragraph alignment

NOTE: Don't place inverted commas (quotation marks) around the align values (i.e. left, center, right). The browser may disregard it and align your paragraph as default.

Adding Spaces

If you type in some text in your body tag and put in **more than one** space between any two words, you will see that when you open the page in the browser the extra spaces have disappeared and there is only **one** space. In HTML, if you want to add more than one space, you have to type **nbsp;** for every extra space you want to insert.

Type in the following and save it as "intspace.html":

```
<HTML>
<HEAD>
<TITLE>
Adding spaces
</TITLE>
</HEAD>
<BODY>
There should be two spaces between do and it.  You have to DO   IT.
</BODY>
</HTML>
```

You should now see the screen shown in Figure 2.6

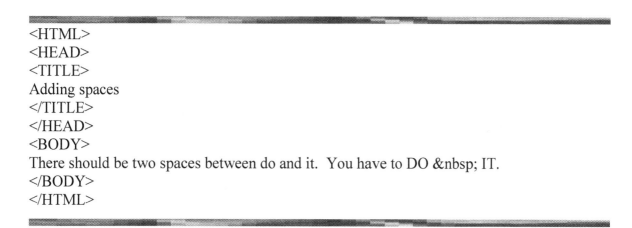

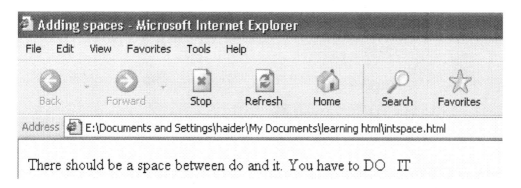

FIGURE 2.6: Inserting more than one space in text

Remember: The first space you enter after a word will always appear. You only need to use **nbsp;** for the extra spaces that you want to insert. Also note that the semi-colon after **nbsp** is also part of the tag. If you don't type it in, then you will just see nbsp written on the web page and no extra spaces will be inserted.

Adding a new line

By now, you will have also found out that if you pressed the enter key and typed in text on a new line in Notepad, this does not show the text in different lines when you view it in the browser. To add new lines, you also need to use a tag. It is almost like a typewriter. You must use the <br> tag

Type in the following code into Notepad and save the file as "lines.html":

```
<HTML>
<HEAD>
<TITLE>
Adding lines
</TITLE>
```

30

```
</HEAD>
<BODY>
This is the first line <BR>
This is the second line
</BODY>
</HTML>
```

Shown in Figure 2.7 is a screenshot of what you should see when you view the web page in a browser.

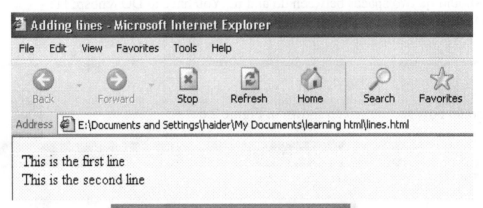

FIGURE 2.7: Inserting line breaks

NOTE: This tag also does not have a closing/ending tag. That means that you don't have to type </BR>. Most of the tags in HTML do have closing tags but the BReak tag is one of the few exceptions.

Typewriter text

This tag will make the text appear as if it were written using a typewriter.
Type in the following code and save the file as "typewriter.html":

```
<HTML>
<HEAD>
<TITLE>
Type writer text
</TITLE>
</HEAD>
<BODY>
<TT>This tag will make the text look like it was typed with a typewriter. </TT>
</BODY>
</HTML>
```

Opening the page in the browser should produce the screen shown in Figure 2.8

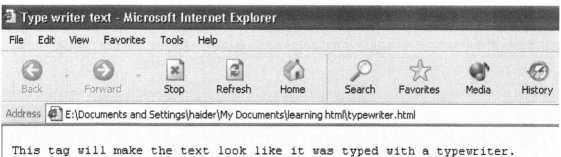

This tag will make the text look like it was typed with a typewriter.

FIGURE 2.8: Typewriter text

Bold text

If you want to make text bold in HTML, you can't just open Notepad and paste in text that is already bold. The web browser will merely display the text as normal text. As you should already know, the same applies to changing font color, size, etc. All of these have to be specified. The tag shown below is used to make text bold.

<B>text that should be bold goes here. </B>

If you want to make only a few words bold, all you have to do, is insert the <B> before the first word you want to make bold and then type </B> after the last word you want to make bold. For example:

<B>**This will be bold**</B> This will not.

Below is an example of the HTML code (known as the **source code)** for a web page which has the first line displayed as bold. Type the code into a Notepad file and save it as "boldtxt.html".

NOTE: Do not forget to type in the ".html" at the end. As I have tried to reiterate, it is called the extension of the file. It tells the browser that the file is a web page and not a text document. If you do not type in the extension (i.e. .html), the web browser will not be able to open the file as it will not know that it is a web page file.

```
<HTML>
<HEAD>
<TITLE>
BOLD TEXT
</TITLE>
</HEAD>
<BODY>
<B> This first sentence should appear as bold text but the second line shouldn't. </B>
HTML can be tedious to learn and type but it is all worth it when you make your first
web page.
</BODY>
</HTML>
```

You should now see the screen shown in Figure 2.9

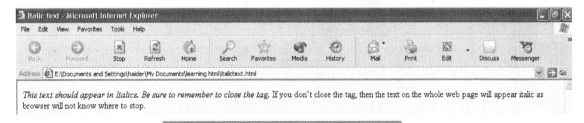

This first line should appear as bold text but the second line shouldn't. HTML can be tedious to learn and type but it is all worth it when you make your first web page.

FIGURE 2.9: Bold text

Italic text

Italicizing text also follows a similar rule to the one used to make text bold. Italicizing text requires you to type in the Italics tag as shown below.

<I>_text between this tag will be shown as italic text_**</I>**

Again, if you only wish to make some of the text italic, just enclose the requisite portion between <I> and </I>

The following example shows a web page which has the first sentence italicized. Type in the code into a Notepad file and save it as "italictxt.html":

```
<HTML>
<HEAD>
<TITLE>
Italic text
</TITLE>
</HEAD>
<BODY>
<I> This text should appear in Italics.  Be sure to remember to close the tag.  </I>
If you don't close the tag, then the text on the whole web page will appear italic as
browser will not know where to stop.
</BODY>
</HTML>
```

Viewing the code in a browser should produce the screen shown in Figure 2.10

This text should appear in Italics. Be sure to remember to close the tag. If you don't close the tag, then the text on the whole web page will appear italic as browser will not know where to stop.

FIGURE 2.10: Italic text

Preformatted text

This is the last text formatting technique we will cover in this chapter. If you use this tag in a webpage, it will make the text appear exactly the way you typed it, showing all the spaces you added and all the paragraphs etc... without the need for using the <P> and <BR> tags, etc.

Type the following code in Notepad and save it as "preformatted.html"

```
<HTML>
<HEAD>
<TITLE>
Preformatted text
</TITLE>
</HEAD>
<BODY>
<PRE>
The text typed should be displayed exactly the way it is written in the source code.  There
should be two spaces after this full stop

          And now a new paragraph                    and several spaces then a
  new line displayed on the webpage.
</PRE>
</BODY>
</HTML>
```

If you typed the source code the way it is written above or at least something similar (in terms of the spaces and indents), your webpage should look like the screenshot shown in Figure 2.11

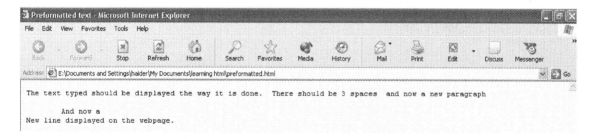

FIGURE 2.11: Preformatted text

Note: If you only want, say a few lines, to appear the way you type them. Then you can add an end tag, i.e. </PRE> after the last word that should appear as it is typed.

EXERCISE 2:

1) Make a webpage which contains information about your favorite sport. Divide the text into three paragraphs.

2) Make a webpage in Arial font and in blue color and size 5 which contains the following lines:
   Even though it may be hard at first to remember all the tags of HTML, it will all become easier with practice.

3) Make a webpage which has the title HTML and in the body contains the following text. Write them as preformatted text. Make the last line into typewriter text.
   Please don't copy and paste all the HTML code that I give you, retype it yourself, this will give you practice. Even if you think you understand, you will just forget it all if you don't try it for yourself.
   Make sure you understand all the tags.

4) Enter the following text as your body
   Inserting spaces may seem a little hard but it only requires a bit of practice to remember it. If you are wish, you can just use the preformatted text tag and then you won't have to insert new paragraphs, lines or spaces using tags. When you use the preformatted text tag, everything that you type in Notepad will appear exactly the same way when you view it in the browser (i.e. the spaces, paragraphs, indents will all appear as they were when typed in Notepad.

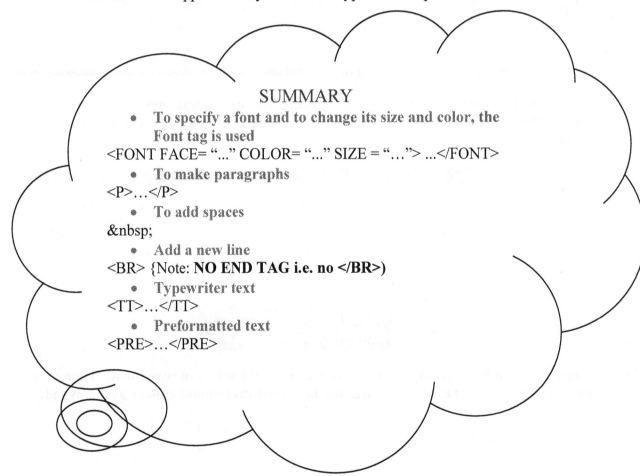

SUMMARY
- To specify a font and to change its size and color, the Font tag is used
  <FONT FACE= "..." COLOR= "..." SIZE = "...> ...</FONT>
- To make paragraphs
  <P>...</P>
- To add spaces

- Add a new line

 {Note: **NO END TAG i.e. no </BR>)**
- Typewriter text
  <TT>...</TT>
- Preformatted text
  <PRE>...</PRE>

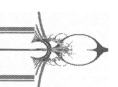

In the last chapter, we looked at how to format text in different ways and how to get some control over its layout. In this chapter we will be looking at how to change the color of the background, how to use an image as a background and how to insert an image into the web page (when it is not supposed to be the background itself). We will also look at how to resize images and position them where we want them along with a few other things.

Now that you have learned some of the very basic instructions, I am going to start off this chapter by reviewing and introducing some html terms.

So let's begin.

a) The first word that follows the "<" sign is called an **element**. It is also commonly known as the **flag**

For example:

    1) <FONT>; FONT is the element.
    2) <BODY>; BODY is the element.

b) An **attribute** is more or less a property or category of an element. For example:

1) <FONT **FACE** = "Arial" **SIZE** = "1" **COLOR** = "Red">. **FACE, SIZE, COLOR** are the attributes.

Some things you should know and remember

    1) HTML is not case-sensitive. That means that the HTML **tags and attribute (including there values)** can be written in either upper-case (capital letters) or lower-case (small letters). For example: <FONT>, or <FONT> or even <FonT> is acceptable. **However:**
    ➤ If you wrote <FONTS…> instead of FONT, the browser will not understand that you typed the "**S**" mistakenly, it will just disregard the tag and your font attributes will not be applied to the text.
    ➤ If you wrote <FONT FACE = "Time New Roman"> instead of "Time**s** New Roman", the browser will again disregard this statement and in turn the text font will not be changed to Times New Roman.
    ➤ If you wrote <FONT COLOUR= "blue"> instead of "color" (No 'U'), then the browser will once again not understand what you are trying to do and in turn the attribute will be disregarded and the text will be displayed in the default color (black).

2) HTML tags can be mixed together. If you type:

<U><I><B>this text will be bold, italic and underlined. </I></U></B>
(The end tags for each of the start tags can be placed in any order. It is not essential to set them out in the same sequence as the beginning tags. However, I would recommend it as it would be easier for you to debug your code. Forming ordered pairs of tags is part of efficient coding.)

3) If you do misspell a tag or forget to place the end tag, it may cause problems with the whole page. If for example, you forget to end the <TITLE > tag, the browser may take the whole body text to be the page's title. Note that how a browser responds to the different errors in coding depends on which browser you use to view your webpage.

HTML TIPS:

- **Try to space out your work neatly.**
- **You should ALWAYS use lower-case. This is due to the fact that the so called next generation of HTML (i.e. XHTML; eXtensible Hyper Text Markup Language) MUST be written in lower-case as it is case-sensitive. Therefore, it is a good idea to practice writing HTML as lower case so that if you decide to learn XHTML, you won't face any problems.**
- **Place comments at different intervals so that it is easier for you to identify the different parts of the webpage when you are updating. NOTE: You will be taught later how to place COMMENTS.**

Changing the background color

In order to change the color of the background of your web page, all you need to do is add an **attribute** to the BODY tag as follows:

<BODY **bgColor**="green">

bgColor tells the browser that we are talking about the background color of the page and the color that you type in quotation marks tells the browser to change the background color to green, etc.

Type the following code in Notepad and save it as "backgroundcol.html":

```
<HTML>
<HEAD>
<TITLE>
Background color changing
</TITLE>
</HEAD>
<BODY bgColor= "green">
The background color for this page should be green.
 </BODY>
</HTML>
```

NOTE: You will have noticed that bgColor was written in lower case and 'C' was left capitalized. This tag can also be written as BGCOLOR, however, if it is typed in lower case, the 'C' MUST be capitalized.

Please note that as stated in the introduction, at the time when the book was sent to the publisher, the intention was to publish the entire book in color. However due to certain logistics that arose in the last minute, the book interior had to be published in black and white. Thus for the reader's convenience, I have uploaded the pages where color is important on the following website:

http://www.wbook.info

Readers can go to the above website and download the relevant sections in color.

Figure 3.0 shows a screenshot of the web page that the above code would produce.

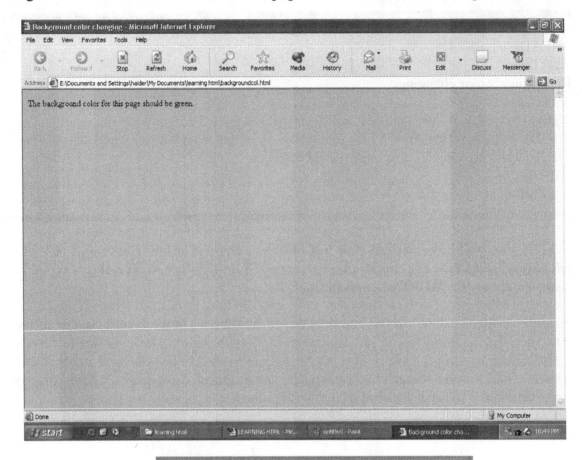

FIGURE 3.0: Changing the background color
of a web page

NOTE: The end tag for any tag ALWAYS has a right slash "/" after the "<". The same applies even if you add attributes to a tag (i.e. the end tag will still have a right slash followed by the element). This applies to ALL tags.

Changing the background color (displaying the different shades)

If you practised changing the background color, you may have noticed that if you typed in, for example, "**dark** green", "**light** green" or just "green" it produced the same color (i.e. with no difference in intensity). Displaying different **shades** of colors is not possible using the above outlined method. In order to get the different shades, the attribute (BGCOLOR) is still used, but the value of the color is given in **hexadecimal**. The way it works is that instead of you typing in a color name, you type in 6 digits. Each two digit pair represents one of the three primary colors of *light* (**R**ed, **G**reen and **B**lue), **RGB**. When dealing with *paint*, the primary colors are red, yellow and blue. *However*, since we are dealing with *light*, the three basic colors are different. For this reason, mixing all the colors will give you white rather than black (as you would expect with paints). Mixing the three primary colors of light allows you to produce millions of different color combinations. The first pair tells the browser what intensity of red is required, the second pair tells the browser how much green to use and the third pair tells the browser the amount of blue you want in the new color (i.e. **RRGGBB)**. You specify the colors using a range between 00-FF (for each color). This method allows you to create all the different colors available. Below is an example:

<BODY BGCOLOR = "#000000">

Note: You should always place a hash (pound) sign (i.e. #) before the RGB values.

If you use "000000", it tells the browser to use "00" red, i.e. *no* red at all; "00" green, i.e. *no* green at all; "00" blue, i.e. *no* blue at all. Therefore, "#000000" will result in the background color being black.

.

"#FFFFFF" is RGB for white.
If you use "#00FF00", it will result in the background color being *bright* green.
Similarly, if you use "#FF0000", it will result in the background color being *bright* red.
As you will have guessed, "#0000FF" will give a *bright* blue background.

In order to produce other colors, all you have to do is use different intensities of each of these colors. For example:

#FF2233 → Dull pink
#aa4911 → bright brown

Fortunately, you don't have to experiment for hours to find the right color; there are *many* web sites on the Internet which tell you the color combinations for hundreds of different colors.

Two of these websites are:
http://www.e-pixs.com/colors2.html
http://www.netkontoret.dk/htmlhexcolors.htm

The colors produced by the different combinations depend on the computers operating system (e.g. Windows, Linux, etc) and on the browser that you use to preview the page. There are **216** colors that will appear the same no matter what browser you use to view them with. These colors are the ones that have been made using a combination of **00, 33, 66, 99, CC** and **FF**. The colors produced using these combinations are termed "**Browser safe colors**".

Remember there are *only* **216** browser safe colors.

Important Note: Font color can also be specified using RGB (i.e. <FONT COLOR= "#000000"> This will produce black text. All the same rules apply to changing the font color using this method. </FONT>)

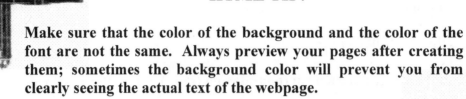

HTML TIP:

Make sure that the color of the background and the color of the font are not the same. Always preview your pages after creating them; sometimes the background color will prevent you from clearly seeing the actual text of the webpage.

Using a picture as the background

The 'Background' attribute is used to insert a picture as the background:

<BODY BACKGROUND = "imgname.jpg">

The image file must be in the same folder as the web page file. It can also be in a subfolder of the folder where the web page file is saved. If you have the image in a sub folder, then type in the <BODY BACKGROUND = "subfolder name/image name.extension"

NOTE: The background image becomes tiled if it is not large enough to cover the whole screen.
Make sure you insert the quotation marks. Write the name of the image you want as the background between the quotation marks. Make sure you type in the extension of the image file that you are using.

If you do not know how to find the extension of a file, refer to the next section.
The following is an example of the source code for a webpage which makes use of the image shown in Figure 3.1 as its background.

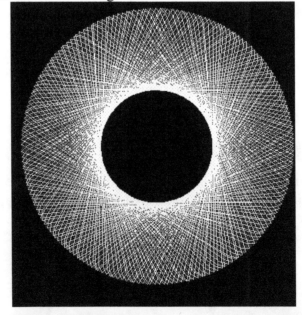

FIGURE 3.1: Using a picture as a background image

41

Type in the following code into Notepad and save the file as "bkimages.html". In this case the image used is called "bkimg.bmp". Replace this with the name of the image that you want to use as the background.

```
<HTML>
<HEAD>
<TITLE>
Background image
</TITLE>
</HEAD>
<BODY BACKGROUND="bkimg.bmp">
<BR>
<BR><BR><BR><BR><BR><BR><BR><BR><BR><BR><BR><BR><BR><BR><B
R><BR><BR><BR>

<FONT COLOR="ff8866">
<PRE>
                    The background image should be <B><I>tiled</I></B>.
</FONT>
</PRE>
</BODY>
</HTML>
```

NOTE: You can also add for example BGCOLOR= "blue" to the BODY tag ('RGB' color is also acceptable). If you do this, the users will see a blue background while the background image is still loading.

Refer to Figure 3.2 for a screenshot of the web page you should see when you view the code in a browser.

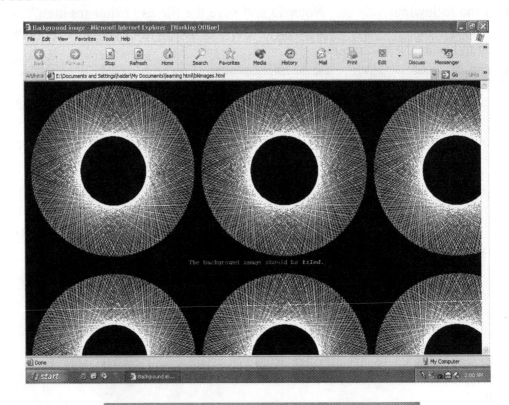

FIGURE 3.2: Changing the background color
of a web page

Please note that as stated in the introduction, at the time when the book was sent to the publisher, the intention was to publish the entire book in color. However due to certain logistics that arose in the last minute, the book interior had to be published in black and white. Thus for the reader's convenience, I have uploaded the pages where color is important on the following website:

http://www.wbook.info

Readers can go to the above website and download the relevant sections in color.

Finding out the extension of image files

Open the folder which contains the image file (Figure 3.3)

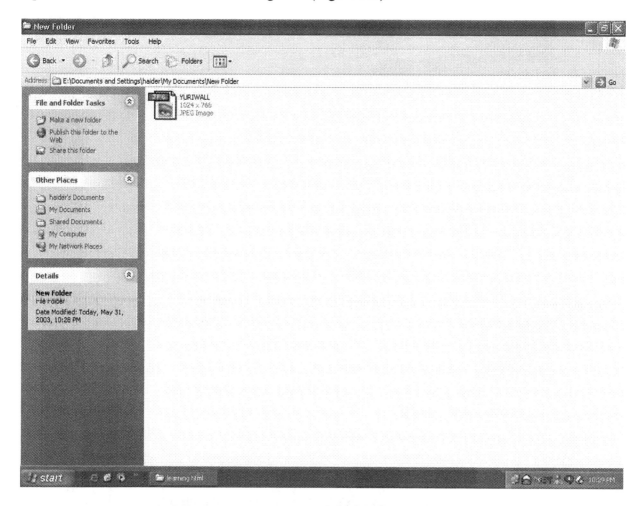

FIGURE 3.3: Folder containing the image file

NOTE: This method can be used to find the extension of any type of file and is not restricted to image files.

Right click on the image file (Figure 3.4)

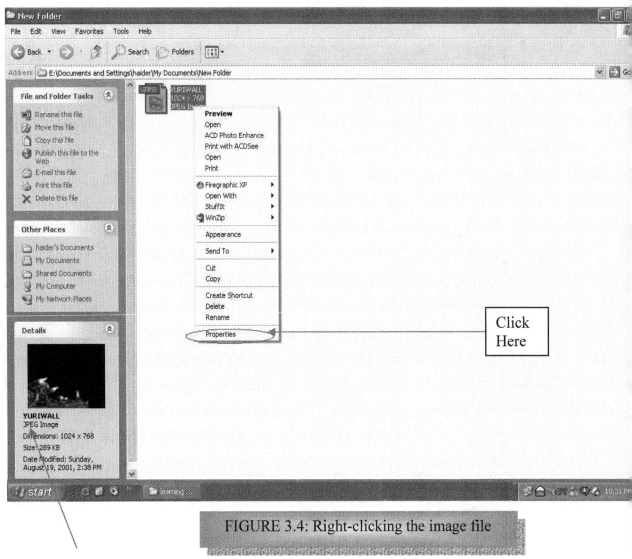

FIGURE 3.4: Right-clicking the image file

Note: Windows XP users will only have to left click on the file. The file extension will be displayed on the bottom left corner.

Click on properties (Figure 3.5)

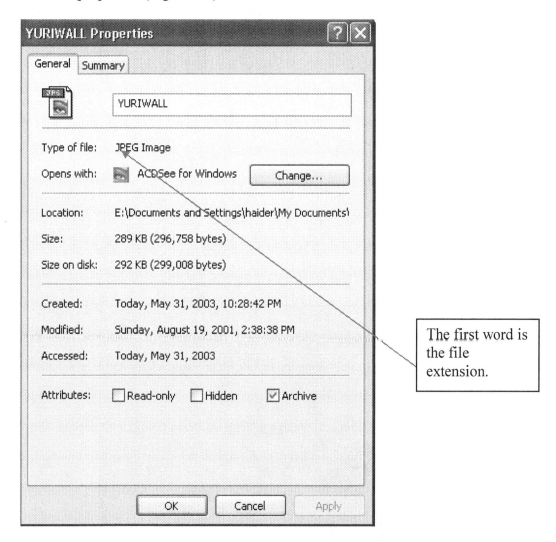

The first word is the file extension.

FIGURE 3.5: Properties of the image file

Inserting an image into a web page

In the previous section, we looked at how to use an image as the background; we will now look at placing an image into the body of the page. This is done as follows:

<IMG SRC = "imagename.extension">

NOTE: This tag does NOT have an end tag.

There isn't much to explain for this tag. **IMG** is the tag. SRC = "imagename.ext" tells the browser the **source** of the image to be displayed on the web page. The image file **MUST** be saved in the same folder as the web page. It can also be saved in a sub-folder (A folder inside the same folder). If for example, your web page is saved in a folder called "HTML" and you have another folder inside it called "images". If the folder, images, contains an image called 'man' and you want to insert this into the web page, then you will have to type in <IMG SRC = "images/man.extension". Note that you don't have to mention the main folder where the web page is stored (i.e. you don't have to type <IMG SRC = "HTML/images/man.extension">).

Remember to type in the extension of the file. Therefore, if the image is saved in a sub-folder, then you have to type in <IMG SRC = "name of folder which contains image/image name.extension".

The following is an example of the source code for a web page which uses the image shown in Figure 3.6 for illustration purposes.

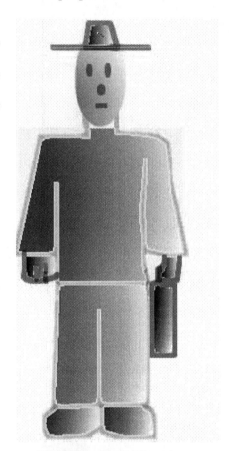

FIGURE 3.6: Image used in the following example web page

Find an image file on your computer; copy it and paste it into a folder. Then type in the following code into Notepad and save the file as "body image.html". **Remember to save the html page in the same folder as the image.** In this case, the image used is "man in suit.bmp". Just replace this with the name of your image file in the source code.

Here is the source code.

```
<HTML>
<HEAD>
<TITLE>
Inserting an image
</TITLE>
</HEAD>
<BODY>
<IMG SRC = "man in suit.bmp">
</BODY>
</HTML>
```

Figure 3.7 shows the web page as it would look in a browser.

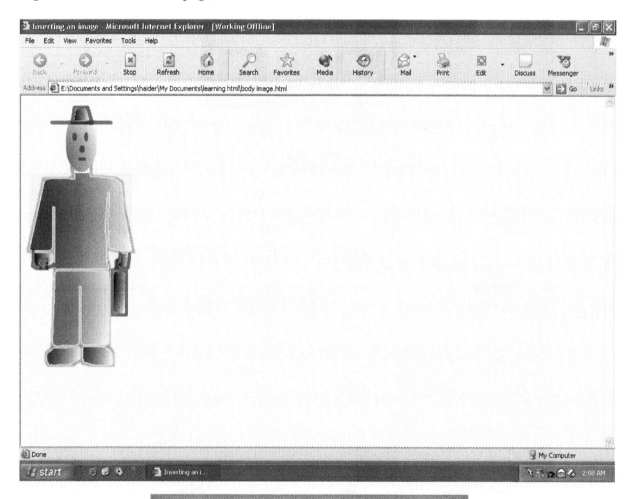

FIGURE 3.6: Adding images to web pages

48

Alternative text for an image

Some browsers don't support images. For this reason, you should specify alternative text for images. It is very easy to do. What happens is that when the user brings the mouse cursor over the image, a pre-written description of the image appears. Below is an example

<IMG SRC = "gardenphoto.bmp" **ALT= "Picture of a garden"**>

The text in the quotation marks is what the person sees when he moves the mouse cursor on top of the image. In line with the philosophy of this book, let us now look at a complete example, which uses the image in Figure 3.7.

FIGURE 3.7: Image that will be used in following web page

The image is that of a cartoon tractor. Find an image file on your computer; copy it and paste it into a folder. Then type in the following code into Notepad and save the file as "alt text.html". **Remember to save the html page in the same folder as the image.** In this case, the image used is "tractor.bmp". Just replace this with the name of your image file in the source code.

```
<HTML>
<HEAD>
<TITLE>
Alternative text for images
</TITLE>
</HEAD>
<BODY>
<IMG SRC = "tractor.bmp" ALT = "Drawing of a tractor">
</BODY>
</HTML>
```

You should see the screen shown in Figure 3.8 when you view the source code in a browser. The "**Drawing of a tractor**" message that can be seen in the screenshot below appears when you keep the cursor stationary over the image for a few seconds. This message has obviously appeared because it was specified using the **ALT** attribute of the **<IMG>** tag.

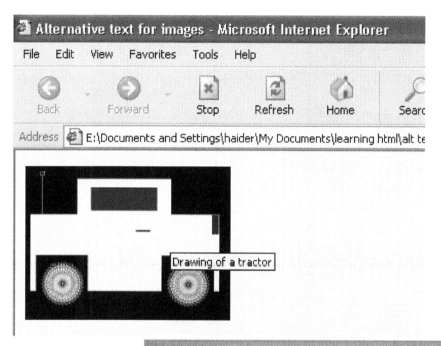

FIGURE 3.8: Specifying alternative text for images

Resizing an image

Using HTML, images can easily be reduced or magnified. You just have to tell the browser what size you want the image to be, and your original image will be minimized or magnified to that specified size. **However**, make sure you don't make the image too big as this will affect the quality of the image. Don't make it too small either so that the details of the image cannot be resolved. Also, ensure that you don't specify a size of say 10 by 50 for a square image. This will **stretch** the image along its width. Make sure you preview your webpage after you add images to it.

Maintain the aspect ratio: this means that you should keep the ratio between the width and the height of the image the same. For example: if you want to halve the size of an image and the original size is width = 20 and height = 40, then you should halve the width (i.e. 10) and halve the height (i.e. 20). If, for example, you specify a width of 20 and a height of 50 for an image which is originally 40 by 40, this will distort the image.

The size (or resolution) of the image is specified in **pixels**. **Pixel** stands for **Pic**ture **Element**; it is an individual dot containing RGB (Red, Green and Blue) values. So how do you find out how many pixels your image is? For Windows XP users, right-click the image file and select Properties. Click on the summary tab (Figure 3.9).

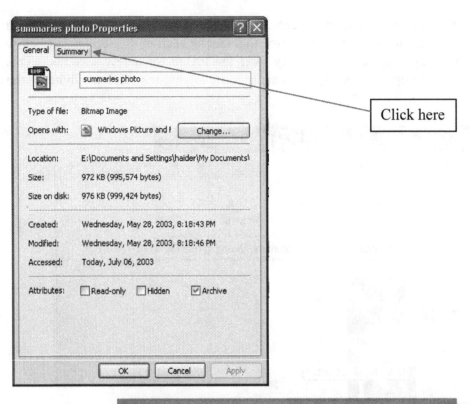

Click here

FIGURE 3.9: Properties for the bitmap image

Click on Advanced (Figure 3.10)

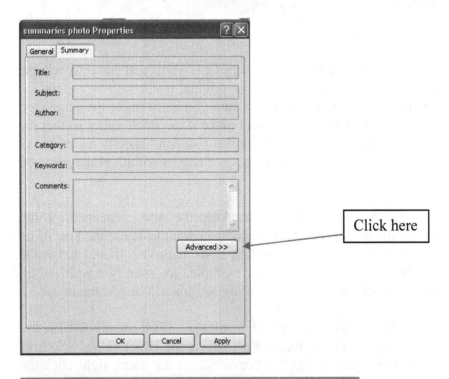

Click here

FIGURE 3.10: Summary tab of properties section

You should now see the screen shown in Figure 3.11 (except obviously with different values for height, width, etc.). The first two fields represent the width and the height of the image.

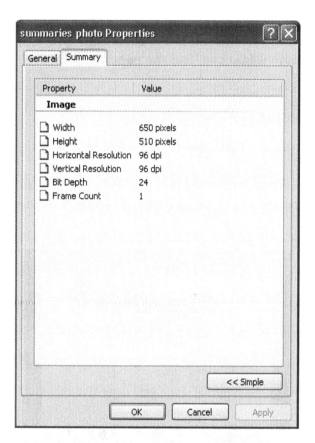

FIGURE 3.11: Summary tab of image properties; advanced settings

You can now better estimate the exact size you need to test values.

Another alternative to this is to open a **graphics program** (example: Paint Shop Pro) and use it to find the width of your image in pixels after you have resized it. Fortunately, you can even use paint. Open Microsoft Paint and paste your image into it. Click on image and select attributes. You will see that you can select pixels in order to view the size of the image.

If this is all too complicated for you and you want to resize your image, use trial and error. Just try out values for the height and width until you obtain the desired size for your image.

NOTE: It is best to resize the images in a graphics program (e.g. Paint) to obtain the required size and save it. This way you don't have to waste time calculating the pixels.

HTML TIP:

If you want your web pages to load faster, you should find the size of your images and include it into the IMG tag. This will decrease the amount of time it takes to load the page.

Now that we have looked at how to find the resolution of your pictures (in pixels), let's look at an example of resizing an image. Figure 3.12 shows the image that we will use in this example:

FIGURE 3.12: Image that will be used in the web page

In this case, we need to decrease the size of the image to half of what it is now. Using the method outlined previously, it was found that this image is 284 pixels wide and 202 pixels high. Therefore in order to halve the size of this image, we need to divide the dimensions by 2 as follows:

Diminished Width = "284 / 2" = 142 pixels

Diminished Height = "202 / 2" = 101 pixels

Therefore, the dimensions of the reduced image will be 142 by 101.

Find an image file on your computer; copy it and paste it into a folder. Then type in the following code into Notepad and save the file as "image dim.html". **Remember to save the html page in the same folder as the image.** In this case, the image used is "image dim.bmp". Just replace this with the name of your image file in the source code.

```
<HTML>
<HEAD>
<TITLE>
Resizing an image
</TITLE>
</HEAD>
<BODY>
<IMG SRC = "image dim.bmp" WIDTH = "142" HEIGHT = "101">
</BODY>
</HTML>
```

Figure 3.13 illustrates the screen that you should see when you view the code in a browser (obviously you would see your own image and not the funny face).

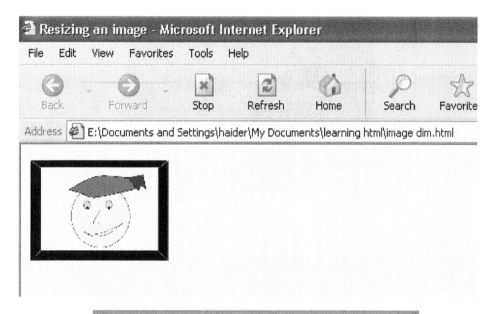

FIGURE 3.13: Resizing an image

Aligning an image

One way you can align images is using the **<P>** tag. It works the same way as for a paragraph of text. You insert the **<p>** tag with the align command specifying how the image should be aligned. Let's look at two examples which align the image shown in Figure 3.14 to the left, center and right of the page.

FIGURE 3.14: Image used in next web page

Find an image file on your computer; copy it and paste it into a folder. Then type in the following code into Notepad and save the file as 'image aligning.html'. **Remember to save the html page in the same folder as the image.** In this case, the image used is "design.bmp". Just replace this with the name of your image file in the source code.

```
<HTML>
<HEAD>
<TITLE>
Aligning images using paragraphs
</TITLE>
</HEAD>
<BODY>
<P ALIGN =left> <IMG SRC= "design.bmp"> </P>

<P ALIGN =center> <IMG SRC = "design.bmp"></P>

</BODY>
</HTML>
```

On viewing the file in a browser, you should see the screenshot shown in Figure 3.15

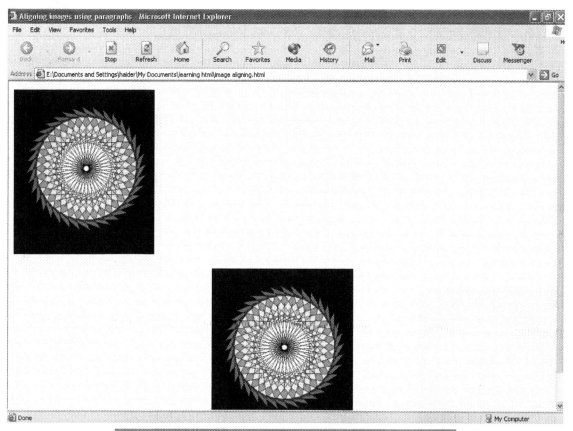

FIGURE 3.15: Aligning images to the left and
center of a web page

Find an image file on your computer; copy it and paste it into a folder. Then type in the following code into Notepad and save the file as 'image aligning1.html'. **Remember to save the html page in the same folder as the image.** In this case, the image used is "design.bmp". Just replace this with the name of your image file in the source code.

```
<HTML>
<HEAD>
<TITLE>
Aligning images using paragraphs
</TITLE>
</HEAD>
<BODY>
<P ALIGN =right> <IMG SRC = "design.bmp"> </P>
<P> <IMG SRC = "design.bmp"> </P>This image should be aligned to the default
position since location has not been specified.
</BODY>
</HTML>
```

When viewed in a browser, you should see the screen shown in Figure 3.16 (obviously with your image on it).

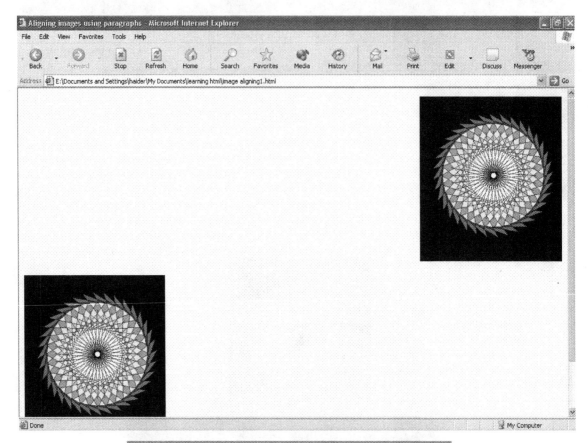

FIGURE 3.16: Aligning images to the right of the web page and default alignment of images

Wrapping text around an image

If you had tried to place some text on the side of an image, you would have noticed that it insisted on having only one line on the side of the image and the rest of the text runs below it. In order to set the position of the text, you have to use the following method.

In order to place the text on the right of the image (starting from the top), you must tell the browser to align the **image** to the left. This is a bit confusing since you want to align the text and yet you have to specify the position of the image. If you tell the browser to align the image to the left, it will align the text on the right and vice versa. If you specify the image to be aligned to the right, the text will automatically be aligned to the left. You can also start the text from the center of the image.

Below is an example which shows the three alignments together. The image used in this example is the same as the one used in one of the previous examples.

Find an image file on your computer which is relatively small in size (particularly its width); copy it and paste it into a folder. Then type in the following code into Notepad and save the file as "text wrap.html". **Remember to save the html page in the same folder as the image.** The image used is "tractor.bmp". Just replace this with the name of your image file in the source code.

```
<HTML>
<HEAD>
<TITLE>
Aligning images using paragraphs
</TITLE>
</HEAD>
<BODY>
<IMG SRC = "tractor.bmp" ALIGN = "left">This text should start from the top of the image and to its right.  If the alignment was not specified, the default would have been used and the text would have started run below the image, with only one line on the right of it.

<BR><BR><BR><BR>
<HR>

<IMG SRC = "tractor.bmp" ALIGN = "right">This text should be on the left of the image.  The text should also start from the top.  The "BR" tag was inserted so that the image of the second tractor does not become aligned to the right of the first one.

<BR><BR><BR><BR>
<HR>

<IMG SRC = "tractor.bmp" ALIGN = "center">This text should be on the right of the image.  The text should start from the center of the image.

<BR>
<HR>

<IMG SRC = "tractor.bmp">This text should be aligned as default (i.e. the first line will be on the right of the image and the rest will run down the image).  As you can see, the text is basically touching the image and it does not look professional.  One simple way to overcome this is to insert a space before the first word.  To find out the right way to do it, read the next section.
</BODY>
</HTML>
```

If you typed in the code properly, you should see the screen as shown in Figure 3.17. Obviously, in your case, you would see the image you specified and not the image of the tractor used in this example.

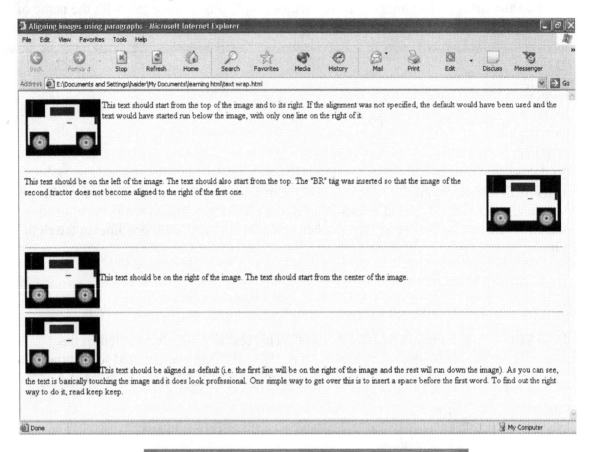

FIGURE 3.17: Wrapping text around images

Horizontal and vertical spacing

You can specify a space around your images where neither text nor images can be placed. The space is specified in terms of vertical space (vspace) and horizontal space (hspace). The dimension of the space is specified in pixels. For example, if you write <IMG SRC = "car.bmp" **hspace = 10 vspace = 10>**, there will be a 10 pixels of space surrounding all sides of the image.

Let's use the same tractor image as above to illustrate the use of creating space around an image. We saw previously that when the tractor image had text next to it, the text was touching the image. This can be overcome by specifying a horizontal space of about 5 pixels around the image. Let's look at the source code for such a page.

Find an image file on your computer which is relatively small in size (particularly its width); copy it and paste it into a folder. Then type in the following code into Notepad and save the file as "hspace.html". The image used is "tractor.bmp". Just replace this with the name of your image file in the source code.

```
<HTML>
<HEAD>
<TITLE>
Horizontal Space around image.
</TITLE>
</HEAD>
<BODY>
<IMG SRC = "tractor.bmp" HSPACE = "5">As you can see, the text is not touching the
image. The reason is that we have specified an invisible layer of 10 pixels along the
horizontal sides of the image. Nothing can be placed in this area.
</BODY>
</HTML>
```

Figure 3.18 shows the code when previewed in a browser.

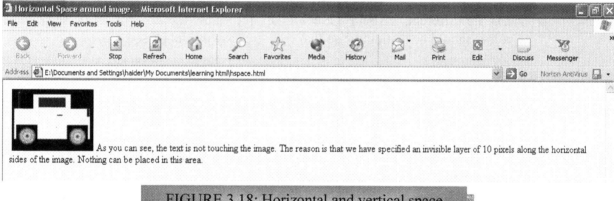

FIGURE 3.18: Horizontal and vertical space
around image

NOTE: The right and left sides of the image are affected by the hspace attribute while the vspace attribute affects the top and bottom of the image.

EXERCISE 3:

1) Define the following terms:
   a) Case-sensitive b) Attribute c) Element d) Flag

2) Make a webpage which has a LIGHT yellow background (Hint: Use hexadecimals to specify the color). Include the following text into the webpage. The text should be red in color and should be displayed as a centered paragraph. The text font should be Arial Black.

   " (Text to be included in body of webpage starts here)

   So far, we have only covered the basics of HTML. If you have any trouble with any part of the book, you should go online and search for a different explanation for what you don't understand. There are hundreds of online tutorials that are available for free online.

   (Text to be included in body of webpage starts here)"

3) Make a web page which has a dark colored picture as its background. Title the page, background pictures. Include the following text into the body of the webpage. Specify white as the color of the text.

   " (Text to be included in body of webpage starts here)

   Always take special care that the color of the background image and the text are different. If both the colors are the same, the text cannot be seen. The colors should be distinctive so that they are easy on the person's eyes.

   (Text to be included in body of webpage starts here)"

4) Make a webpage that has an image with a size of 45 by 50 pixels. The image should also contain alternative text which says, "This image is 45 by 50 pixels". The image must also have a horizontal and vertical spacing around it of 7 pixels. The image should be aligned to the left of the following text. The following text must be bold, italic and underlined:

   " (Text to be included in body of webpage starts here)

   Always specify the width and height of an image within the IMG tag. This makes it quicker for the webpage to load. The browser has to arrange all the content that will be displayed on the webpage and therefore it has to calculate how much space each object will take. This is why specifying the dimensions help the browser since it can read the dimensions from the tag.

   (Text to be included in body of webpage starts here)"

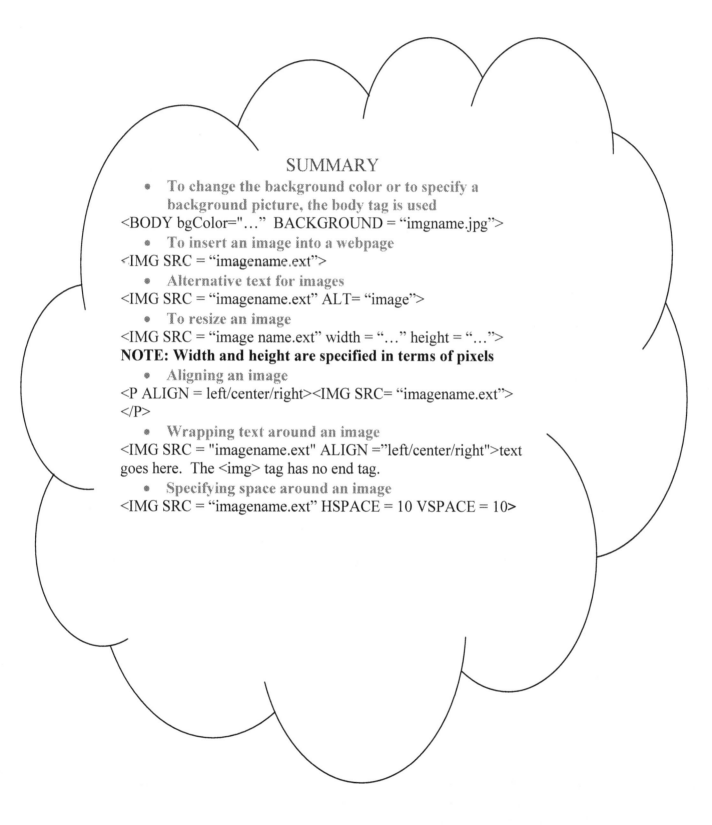

SUMMARY

* To change the background color or to specify a background picture, the body tag is used

<BODY bgColor="..." BACKGROUND = "imgname.jpg">

* To insert an image into a webpage

<IMG SRC = "imagename.ext">

* Alternative text for images

<IMG SRC = "imagename.ext" ALT= "image">

* To resize an image

<IMG SRC = "image name.ext" width = "..." height = "...">

NOTE: Width and height are specified in terms of pixels

* Aligning an image

<P ALIGN = left/center/right><IMG SRC= "imagename.ext"></P>

* Wrapping text around an image

<IMG SRC = "imagename.ext" ALIGN ="left/center/right">text goes here. The <img> tag has no end tag.

* Specifying space around an image

<IMG SRC = "imagename.ext" HSPACE = 10 VSPACE = 10>

This chapter is all about creating links. It will teach you how to create text links to other websites. It will also teach you how to create download links, email links and how to use images as links.

Uniform Resource Locator (URL)

There are billions of web pages on the Internet. Each webpage has a specific address with which it can be accessed. This address is called the uniform resource locator. An example is as follows:

http://www.test.com/index.html

The http:// is the name of the protocol. www.test.com is the name of the domain server. index.html is the name of the file that needs to be retrieved from the server.

When you type in an address, for example, www.google.com, you will notice that you have not specified the name of the file that you wish to access, however, the google homepage still appears. The way it works is that when a user types in the website's address (without specifying a particular file, i.e. no "filename.html" at the end), for example, www.hotmail.com, the server will automatically send back the "**index**.html" file saved on that server. You should note that the URL in the address bar will automatically change to www.hotmail.com/index.html. Therefore, when you upload your webpage onto the web, you *must* make sure that the file which correlates to your homepage of your website is called "**index**.html". Note: It can also be called "**default**.html".

What if you didn't name your homepage file "**index**.html" or "**default**.html" and uploaded all the files of your website onto the server - what file would the browser display when your website's URL is typed without specifying the name of the file at the end? Since the browser will not know which file to retrieve, it will just display a page which lists all the files and directories saved on the server (for that particular website).

Creating Website Links

Creating website links is quite a simple topic; however, few books actually make an effort to clarify the common misconceptions about the workings of a webpage. This usually leaves the reader somewhat baffled leading to further confusion. Let us shed some light on this topic here as to ensure the reader has an adequate understanding of website links.

As an average web user, you probably perceive a website as being just **one** file, where you can click certain links and parts of the page changes. However, this idea of a webpage is untrue and it is now time for a more informed approach. In reality, clicking a link takes you to a "different page" altogether (although there is one exception which is discussed later in this chapter)

Let's start off with a sample webpage. Type in the following source code and save the file as "page1.html"

```
<HTML>
<HEAD>
<TITLE>
Page 1
</TITLE>
</HEAD>
<BODY>
<A HREF = "page2.html"> This link takes you to another page </A>
Links are most commonly used to point to other pages.  Links which take you to a
different section of the same page are not as commonly used.  You may have always
thought that clicking a link merely changes the text on the page, however, in reality it
actually takes you to a different page altogether.
</BODY>
</HTML>
```

After you're done, open a new Notepad document and type in the following source code and name the file "page2.html"

```
<HTML>
<HEAD>
<TITLE>
Page 2
</TITLE>
</HEAD>
<BODY>
As you can see clicking the link brings you to this page.  This page has a different file
name and its own source code.
</BODY>
</HTML>
```

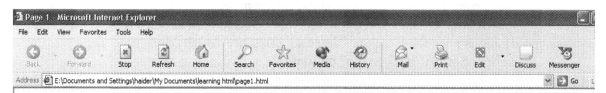

FIGURE 4.1: Page 1

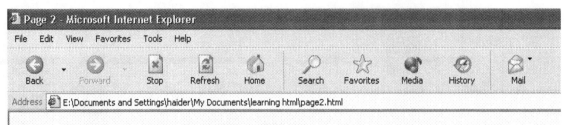

As you can see clicking the link brings you to this page. This page has a different file name and its own source code.

FIGURE 4.2: Page 2

A website can have three types of links. When you click a link on a webpage, it loads up **another** document. It may seem like it is the same document since the navigation and background will usually be the same for both files, however, it is a completely separate document with all parameters of the webpage (e.g. background color, source code, etc.) specified in the source code of the page.

The source code of the webpage contains the URL of the file to load up once a particular link is clicked. .

There are three types of links:

1. **Local links**: When your link directs to another document of your webpage. For example: If your website is www.mysite.com and there is a link on it to a page called www.mysite.com/about.html, this is a local link because "about.html" is just another page of your website.
2. **External links:** When your link leads to a different "website", it is called an external link. For example, if your website is www.mysite.com, and it has a link on it which leads to www.yahoo.com. This is an external link since the link leads to a **different website** altogether whereas in local links, it merely leads to a **different file** on your website's server.
3. **Internal link:** This is the exception: Clicking the link in this case does not take you to a separate document. When a link merely leads to a different section of the **same** page, it is called an internal link. For example, you may have a "table of contents" in the top section of the page followed by the actual content on the same page, whereby you can click on the different sections on the table of contents list It then directly takes you to the relevant selected section and saves you the trouble of having to scroll down. Internal links are usually just used for indexing a webpage or for "back to top" buttons.

This may seem like a lot of information and may even be difficult to understand at this stage, however, below is a summary of important points:

- Every webpage has a unique URL (Uniform Resource Locator)
- A webpage usually consists of a series of interlinked documents (i.e. it is made up of **several** files). It is *not* just one page. Note: A webpage can merely consist of one file but here we are assuming that the website has some form of linking on its page, like yahoo or hotmail, where when you click on E-mail, or Cars, etc…, you will be taken to a **different** page.
- There are three types of links: **local** – leads to different file of same webpage, **external** – leads to a **different website** altogether and **internal** – leads to a different part of the same file (page). From the three, the concept of internal links will probably seem the most confusing. However, a few examples should help clarify the different types of links.

Common structure of specifying a link

The way you create a link on your website is the same whether it is a local, external or internal link. The general format is as follows:

< A HREF = "www.thewebsite.com"> Click here to go to my site </A>
The **"A"** stands for anchor.
HREF stands for **H**yper **REF**erence. i.e. it tells the browser where the link goes to.
www.thewebsite.com is the website the page will go to upon clicking the link.
Click here to go to my site is the text that will be displayed onto the webpage as the link
</A> is the end tag for the anchor tag

This tag is known as the **anchor** tag. Basically, what you write as the value of the HREF will be the URL the browser goes to upon clicking the link. The text that you want to appear on the page for the link is enclosed with the **anchor** tag.

In browsers, the default color of active links (links that haven't been clicked before) is blue whereas the color of links which have been visited previously is pink. This color, however, can easily be changed using HTML.

Please note that as stated in the introduction, at the time when the book was sent to the publisher, the intention was to publish the entire book in color. However due to certain logistics that arose in the last minute, the book interior had to be published in black and white. Thus for the reader's convenience, I have uploaded the pages where color is important on the following website:

http://www.wbook.info

Readers can go to the above website and download the relevant sections in color.

Local links

An example of local links has been covered previously when talking about the structure of a website as being a series of interlinked documents. However, for practice, let's do another example.

Type in the following code into Notepad and save the file as "locallinkhome.html"

```
<HTML>
<HEAD>
<TITLE>Page with a local link</TITLE>
</HEAD>
<BODY>
<A HREF = "locallinkp2.html"> Click here to go to a different page</A>
</BODY>
</HTML>
```

Then type in the following code into Notepad and save the file as "locallinkp2.html"

```
<HTML>
<HEAD>
<TITLE>
Page with a local link
</TITLE>
</HEAD>
<BODY>
As you can see, this is a separate page altogether.
</BODY>
</HTML>
```

Open "locallinkhome.html" in a browser. Figure 4.3 shows what you should see.

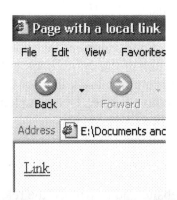

FIGURE 4.3: Page with a local link

Click on Link and you will now be taken to "locallinkp2.html"! (Figure 4.4)

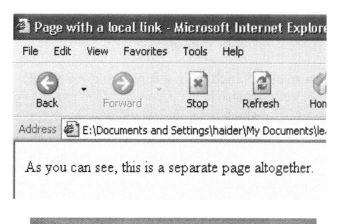

FIGURE 4.4: Link leads to this page

If you now click the back button of your browser:  you will be taken back to "locallinkhome.html". This time, however, the color of "Link" will be pink instead of blue (for Internet explorer users) as shown in Figure 4.5. This is a result of the default settings of the browser. Active links (links which have not been clicked previously are blue in color) and links which have been visited (clicked upon) are pink in color.

FIGURE 4.4: Link is now pink

Local links for websites can either contain the name of the webpage file that it is linking to or the actual website of the file. For example: If my site is called www.sitemainpage.com and I have a link on this page to "subpage.html". I could specify this in two ways, as illustrated below:

Method 1: <A HREF = "subpage.html"> sub page </A>
Method 2: <A HREF = "www.sitemainpage.com/subpage.html>subpage</A>

Method 1 of specifying the link is an example of relative linking and Method 2 is an example of absolute linking.

What if you have your desired file within a subdirectory, can you use relative linking? Yes, all you have to do is:

<A HREF = "subdirectory/page.html"> page </A>

Now the question remains as to which linking approach is preferable. Relative linking is shorter and gives neater code. It also helps if you decide to change your web host (i.e. change the link to the site), in which case, you would have to retype all the links if you had used absolute linking. Another advantage of relative linking is that you can test the links before uploading them to your website (i.e. you can test it locally (offline) on your machine). However, there is a disadvantage to using relative linking which is discussed in the search engine optimization section (bonus section).

The default settings for the colors of active links and visited links can easily be changed by specifying their colors in the body tag. This process is shown below.

Link, alink and vlink

In order to specify your own color for unclicked and visited links, you must use the link and vlink attribute. There is also one other attribute called "alink". When you click on a link, the color of the link changes momentarily while the link is being loaded, this color can be specified using the alink attribute. Note that these settings will apply to local, external and internal links.

Let's look at an example:

Type in the following code and save the file as "lcolour.html"

```
<HTML>
<HEAD>
<TITLE>
alink and vlink
</TITLE>
</HEAD>
<BODY LINK = "GREEN" ALINK = "BLACK" VLINK = "#990005">
<A HREF = "LOCALLINKP2.HTML">Link to the local link example page</A>
</BODY>
</HTML>
```

Figures 4.5, 4.6 and 4.7 show the link before being clicked, while it is clicked and immediately after clicking on the back button of the browser respectively. Note that when you click the back button, the link will still be highlighted so click on the blank in order to unselect it.

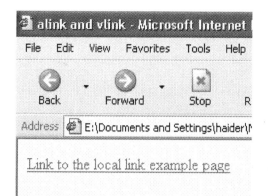

FIGURE 4.5: Link before clicking

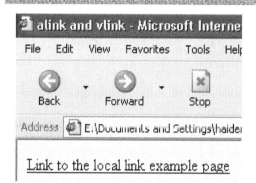

FIGURE 4.6: Link as it is clicked (alink)

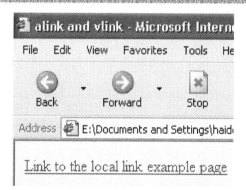

FIGURE 4.7: Link upon returning (vlink)

External links

The basic idea behind all links is similar. The same <a> tag is used to specify external links except this time the URL of the website is stated rather than the actual name of the local file.

Let's create a webpage with a link to www.google.com:

Type in the following code and save the file as "elink.html"

```
<HTML>
<HEAD>
<TITLE>
External links
</TITLE>
</HEAD>
<BODY>
<A HREF = "http://www.google.com"> Go to Google </A>
</BODY>
</HTML>
```

Figure 4.8 shows what you would see when you open the file in a browser:

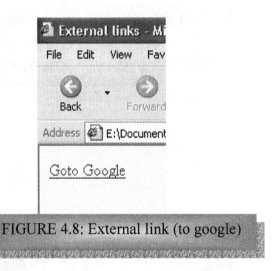

FIGURE 4.8: External link (to google)

On clicking the link, you will be taken to www.google.com (you must be connected to the Internet).

Internal links

Internal links take you to a different section of the same page.

This is best understood with an example:

Type in the following code and save the file as "ilinks.html".

```
<HTML>
<HEAD>
<TITLE>
External links
</TITLE>
</HEAD>
<BODY>
<A HREF = "#bottom"> This link will take you straight to the bottom of the page </a>
<BR><BR><BR><BR><BR><BR><BR><BR><BR><BR><BR><BR><BR><BR>
<BR><BR><BR><BR><BR><BR><BR><BR><BR><BR><BR><BR><BR><BR><B
R><BR><BR><BR><BR><BR><BR><BR><BR><BR><BR><BR><BR><BR>
<BR>
<A ID = "bottom"> This is the bottom of the page</A>
</BODY>
</HTML>
```

Upon clicking the link, the browser should take you to the bottom of the page. (You will not see the page scrolling down; it takes you directly to the bottom of the page). Internal links come in handy for making table of contents pages and back to top buttons. Figure 4.9 and 4.10 show what you should see before and after clicking the link.

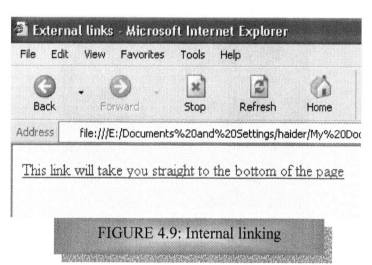

FIGURE 4.9: Internal linking

This is the bottom of the page

Be sure to include the hash sign (#) before the word bottom when referring to that section, otherwise the link will not work.

It is also worth noting that "<a id…" is the same as "<a name…", however, name has been deprecated from the HTML 4.0 specification and has been replaced by "id".

Links using images

In order to use an image as a link, you must merely specify the location of the image in between the <a> and </a> tag.

<A HREF = "pagex.html"> <IMG SRC = "flower.html"> </A>

This code will display an image on the page that has a link to go to "pagex.html".

Let's look at an example:

The image used in this case is shown below. It is called "fractal" and is a bmp file.

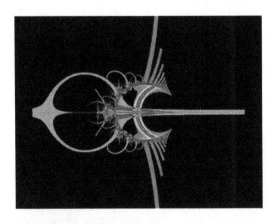

Type in the following code and save the file as "imagelinks.html". Use your own image instead and replace "fractal.bmp" with the name of the image you use.

```
<HTML>
<HEAD>
<TITLE>
Image as a link
</TITLE>
</HEAD>
<BODY>
<A HREF = "www.fractals.com"><IMG SRC = "fractal.bmp" WIDTH = "250"
HEIGHT = "150"></A>
</BODY>
</HTML>
```

Figure 4.11 shows what you should see when you view the page in a browser:

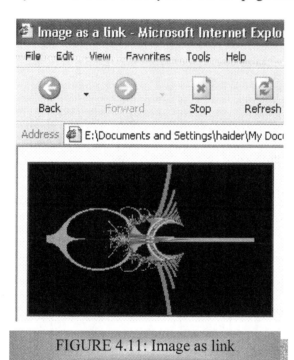

FIGURE 4.11: Image as link

Note that there is a blue border around the image. This is due to the fact that it is a link. Can you think of a way to get rid of this border? Just include **border = "0"** in the <img> tag. This will remove the border.

Clicking the link should take you to www.fractals.com

74

Email link

The very basic structure for inserting an e-mail link is as follows: Clicking the link will open the users default email client with your e-mail address in the address bar.

The format of an e-mail tag is:

<A HREF = "MAILTO: email@provider.com"> Click here to email me </A>

Let's look at the full code for this page. Type in the following into Notepad and save as "mailto.html"

```
<HTML>
<HEAD>
<TITLE>
Email links
</TITLE>
</HEAD>
<BODY>
<A HREF = "MAILTO:email@provider.com"> Click here to email me</A>
</BODY>
</HTML>
```

You should see the screen shown in Figure 4.12 when you view the page in the browser

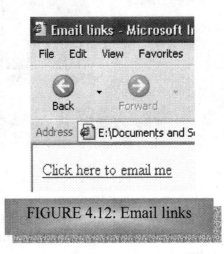

FIGURE 4.12: Email links

Clicking the link opens the default e-mail client on the computer. In my case, this is Microsoft Outlook. If you have Microsoft Outlook too, you should see the screen shown in Figure 4.13

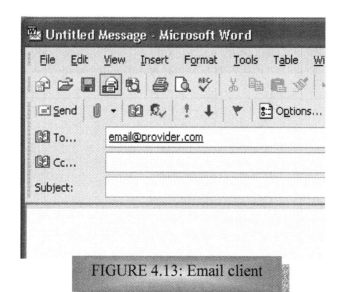

FIGURE 4.13: Email client

Download links

Use the <a> tag. For example: If you want a download link for "www.site.com/tut.zip", then type: <A HREF = "www.site.com/tut.zip"> Click to download </A>

EXERCISE 4:

1) Differentiate between the terms local, external and internal links.
2) Create a webpage called "index.html". On this page, add links to files called "page1.html", "page2.html" and "page3.html". Name the links as appropriate. Now create files called "page1.html", "page2.html" and "page3.html". Place a link back to the "index.html" page on each of these. Now test all the links to make sure they work.
3) Take the web pages created in the previous question to a new level and turn into something more meaning full. Use these files as the basis for a website with four pages. Make the webpage related to any topic you please.
4) Change the alink, vlink and link values for the links on the web pages you have just created to yellow, green and black respectively. Do you think these are appropriate colors to use?
5) Place an e-mail link at the bottom of "index.html".

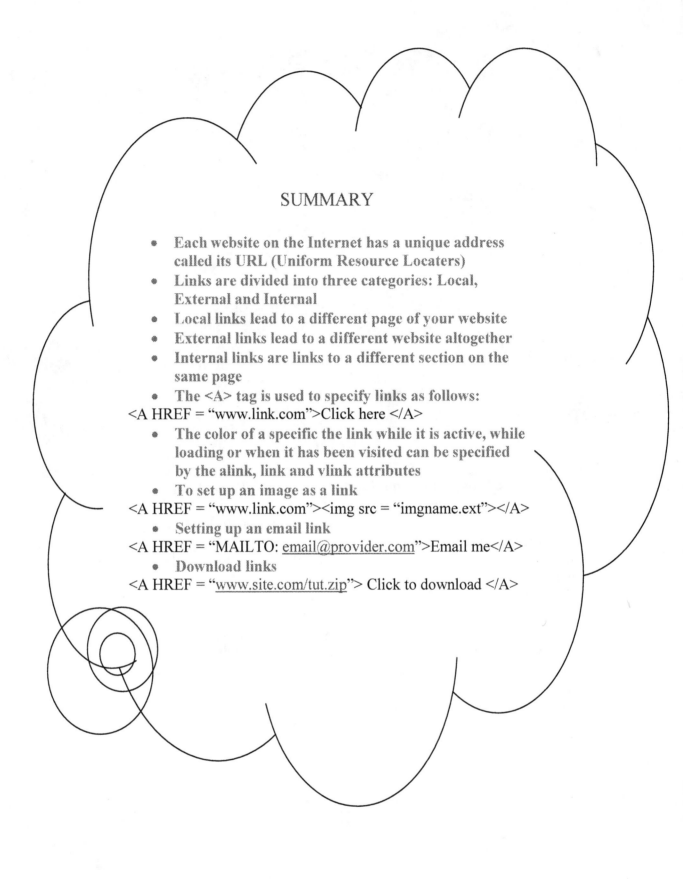

SUMMARY

- Each website on the Internet has a unique address called its URL (Uniform Resource Locaters)
- Links are divided into three categories: Local, External and Internal
- Local links lead to a different page of your website
- External links lead to a different website altogether
- Internal links are links to a different section on the same page
- The <A> tag is used to specify links as follows:

<A HREF = "www.link.com">Click here </A>

- The color of a specific the link while it is active, while loading or when it has been visited can be specified by the alink, link and vlink attributes
- To set up an image as a link

<A HREF = "www.link.com"><img src = "imgname.ext"></A>

- Setting up an email link

<A HREF = "MAILTO: email@provider.com">Email me</A>

- Download links

<A HREF = "www.site.com/tut.zip"> Click to download </A>

Tables are very useful for formatting the layout of a page. However, tables are considered as advanced HTML and are beyond the scope of this book for the most part, as this book is primarily aimed at beginners. For this reason, I will only introduce tables in this chapter. You will note that this chapter does not provide as many screenshots and examples of the different codes. You are advised to try out the different codes for yourself in order to see the results first hand. At the end of this chapter, I have specified links to some online tutorials that contain more information on tables. These should teach you more about working with advanced tables.

The idea behind tables is that a section of the page or the whole page itself is divided into rows and columns.

I have intentionally not included a summary at the end of this chapter. There are a substantial number of tags and attributes that are covered in the chapter and I deemed it necessary for the reader to be acquainted with them adequately without having to filter some of them out. Thus I believe that the chapter in itself is a self-contained unit that does not require a summary per se. A summary would have to be unnecessarily detailed so getting used to the various tags and attributes mentioned in this chapter is in the reader's best interest if they wish to utilize tables for their web designing.

Let's start off by looking at an example:

<TABLE BORDER = "2"> ←Starts off the table and border shows the outline of the table. The higher the number the thicker the outline.
<TR> ← Starts the first row
<TD> ← Starts the first column in the row
This is the text that will appear on the first row
</TD> ← Ends the first column
</TR> ← Ends the first row
</TABLE> ← Ends the table

This code would be typed in the body of the html document and the result would be as shown in Figure 5.1

This is the text that will appear on the first row

FIGURE 5.1: Simple table

Inserting more columns

<TABLE BORDER = "0"> ←Starts off the table. No border this time
<TR> ← Starts the first row
<TD> ← Starts the first column in the row
Column 1
</TD>
<TD> ← Starts the second column in the row
Column2
</TD>
<TD>
Column 3
</TD>
</TR> ← Ends the first row
</TABLE> ← Ends the table

When you enter the above code into the body section of the file, save the file and preview it in the browser, you should see the following table shown in Figure 5.2

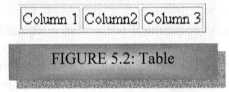

| Column 1 | Column2 | Column 3 |

FIGURE 5.2: Table

The three boxes are actually referred to as cells.

You can insert an image into a cell by merely typing in the image location within the <TD> tag:

<TD>
<IMG SRC = "imagename.ext">
</TD>

You can format the image any way you wish. You can set a width and border, etc. just as you would do if it were an image on the page.

Formatting the table

There are four basic attributes for the table tag:
BORDER = X → specifies the thickness of the border
CELLSPACING = X → this specifies how much space there should be between the cell border and the contents of the cell.
CELLPADDING = X → this specifies how much white space there must be between **cells**.
All of these attributes are typed within the actual <table> tag (not the <TD> or <TR> tag).

Caption

This tag is simple enough to understand. If you want to have a caption for a table which will be displayed **above** the table (not in a cell), use the <caption> tag. The tag is placed after the <table> tag. For example:

```
<TABLE BORDER = "2">
<CAPTION> Useless numbers </CAPTION>
<TR>
  <TD> 1 </TD>  <TD> 2 </TD>
</TR>
</TABLE>
```

Setting up an empty cell

In order to have an empty cell, one would think that you would just set up the table as usual and not write anything between the <TD> start and end tags. This, however, would produce the following result (Figure 5.3)

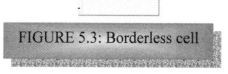

FIGURE 5.3: Borderless cell

In this case, the empty cell will not have any visible borders even if you specified the border as being say "4". This is not the correct method of leaving a cell blank.

The proper method of setting up a blank table cell is by entering   in between the <TD> tag. i.e.

<TD>   <TD> → Correct method → [   ]

<TD> <TD> → Wrong method → [   ]

Colspan

Say you wanted to create a table such as the one shown in Figure 5.4, how would you do it? At first, you may think, well, that's simple enough to do but upon closer inspection you will notice that the cell which holds the word **Sales** actually spans two columns, i.e. there are two columns below it.

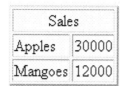

Sales	
Apples	30000
Mangoes	12000

FIGURE 5.4: Use of the <rowspan> tag

So, now you think, well, you could just set an empty column on the right of the sales cell and then decrease its width to an unnoticeable amount. This, however, is not possible since decreasing the column width would also decrease the width of the column below it.

80

In order to have a cell spanning two column widths, you must use the <colspan> tag. Let's look at an example:

```
<HTML>
<BODY>
<TABLE BORDER = "2">
<TR>
<TD COLSPAN = "2" ALIGN = "center"> Sales </TD>
</TR>
<TR>
 <TD> Apples </TD>
  <TD> 30000 </TD>
</TR>
<TR>
  <TD> Mangoes </TD>
  <TD> 12000 </TD>
</TR>
</TABLE>
</BODY>
</HTML>
```

The above code will produce the table shown in Figure 5.4. Notice that the word **Sales** could be formatted any way we wanted using the standard html tags for formatting text. For example, it could be made bold, italic, underlined and could aligned to the right or left of the cell. Try to alter the formatting of the Sales cell to get some practice with tables.

Let's look at the <colspan> tag more closely:

<TD colspan = "2">
The number **2** specifies the number of columns the cell is to span. If it were 10, the cell would span across 10 cells.

The general form of the tag could therefore be written as:

<TD colspan = "x"> where "x" is a positive integer.

It is important to note that I have not covered other similar tags used with tables: <thead>, <tfoot> and <tbody> as these tags are currently not supported by many browsers. The <colspan> tag can also be used with the <thead> tag.

81

Rowspan

This works on the same principle as the <colspan> tag. The only difference being that it allows a cell to span across several **rows** whereas colspan allows spanning across several **columns**.

Let's look at an example to learn how to use the rowspan tag. Type in the code shown below into Notepad and save the file as "rowspan.html"

```
<HTML>
<HEAD> <TITLE> Grades Table </TITLE></HEAD>

<BODY>
<TABLE BORDER = "3" CELLPADDING = "3" CELLSPACING = "2">
<CAPTION><FONT SIZE = " 4" COLOR = "#011794"> <B>Grades</B>
</FONT></CAPTION>

<TR>
  <TD ROWSPAN = "4"> <FONT COLOR = "#011794"> <B> Advanced Subsidiary
</B></FONT> </TD>
  <TD> Physics </TD> <TD> A </TD>
</TR>

<TR>
  <TD> Chemistry </TD> <TD> B </TD>
</TR>

<TR>
  <TD> Computer Studies </TD> <TD> C </TD>
</TR>

<TR>
  <TD> Math </TD> <TD> A </TD>
</TR>

<TR>
  <TD ROWSPAN = "4"> <FONT COLOR = "#011794"> <B> <center>Advanced-level
</center> </B>

</TD>
  <TD> Physics </TD> <TD> D </TD>

<TR>
  <TD> Chemistry </TD> <TD> A </TD>
</TR>

<TR>
  <TD> Computer Studies </TD> <TD> E </TD>
</TR>
```

```
<TR>
  <TD> Math </TD> <TD> A </TD>
</TR>

</TABLE>
</BODY>
</HTML>
```

Note that this example also illustrates the use of the cellpadding and cellspacing tag. It is also an example of formatting the cells of tables. Make sure that you type this example out and try to change different attribute values as it would serve as good practice.

If you typed in the above code and viewed the page in a browser, the table you should see is shown in Figure 5.5

Grades

	Physics	A
Advanced Subsidiary	Chemistry	B
	Computer Studies	C
	Maths	A
Advanced-level	Physics	D
	Chemistry	A
	Computer Studies	E
	Maths	A

FIGURE 5.5: Use of the <colspan> tag

Table width

The width of tables can be specified in terms of pixels or as a percentage of the whole page. The width of the table is specified in the <table> tag using the width attribute.

For example: <TABLE WIDTH = "100%> ...</TABLE>
This table would be displayed across the whole page. If the width of the table is specified in terms of pixels, the table might appear differently when viewed in different resolutions. An 800 pixel wide table might appear fine on a 1024 by 786 monitor screen but it would go beyond the width of the page if viewed at a resolution of 640 by 480.

The relative percentages of the columns can also be set using the width attribute in the <TD> tag. An example of this can be seen in the next section.

Tables are widely used to set up navigation bars for web pages and some web pages are completely based on tables.

We will now look at how tables could be used to set up navigation menus for a website.

Tables as Navigation Menus

A navigation menu is very easy to make using tables. All you have to do is set up a table with one row and as many columns as you like.

Let's consider an example. Type in the following code into Notepad and save the file as "tabnavmenu.html":

```
<HTML>
<HEAD>
<TITLE>Navigation menu using tables</TITLE>
</HEAD>

<BODY  TOPMARGIN="0" RIGHTMARGIN="0" LEFTMARGIN="0"
MARGINWIDTH="0" MARGINHEIGHT = "0" BGCOLOR = "BLACK"
TEXT="WHITE">

<TABLE BORDER = "2" BORDERCOLOR = "RED" BGCOLOR = "BLACK" WIDTH
= "100%" HEIGHT = "3.5%">
<TR>
<TD WIDTH = "20%"> <CENTER><B>Link 1</B></CENTER></TD>
<TD WIDTH = "20%"> <CENTER><B>Link 2</B></CENTER></TD>
<TD WIDTH = "20%"> <CENTER><B>Link 3</B></CENTER></TD>
<TD WIDTH = "20%"> <CENTER><B>Link 4</B></CENTER></TD>
<TD WIDTH = "20%"> <CENTER><B>Link 5</B></CENTER></TD>
</TR>
</TABLE>

</BODY>
</HTML>
```

When viewed in a browser, you should see the following screen (Figure 5.6)

FIGURE 5.5: Tables as navigation menus

Obviously, the words Link 1, Link 2 ... would be replaced by the appropriate links. i.e.
<A HREF = "www.linkaddress.com"> Link text </A>

The above example illustrates a number of new attributes which are discussed below:

84

TOPMARGIN="0" → This specifies the amount of space there should be between the content of the page and the top of the page.
RIGHTMARGIN="0" → This specifies the amount of space there should be between the right edge of the browser and the content of the page.
LEFTMARGIN="0" → This specifies how much space there should be between the left edge of the browser and the content of the page.
MARGINWIDTH="0" → This specifies how much space there should be between the left edge of the browser and the content of the page.
MARGINHEIGHT = "0" → This specifies the amount of space there should be between the content of the page and the top of the page.

Note that **topmargin** and **marginheight** are the same and **leftmargin** and **marginwidth** are also the same. The reason that they both have to be used is to ensure that your page is compatible with both Internet Explorer and Netscape.

Internet explorer supports the first four attributes while Netscape only supports the last two.

The webpage we have just created is also an example of using percentages in tables. The use of percentages also helped making sure that all the cells were the same width.

Let's expand the example above and create a complete layout for a webpage.

Type in the following code and save the file as "tablayout.html". In this case, some of the HTML code has been typed out in lowercase as it makes it easier to read.

```
<HTML>
<HEAD>
<TITLE>Heading</TITLE>
</HEAD>

<BODY  topmargin="0" rightmargin="0" leftmargin="0" marginwidth="0" marginheight
= "0" bgColor = "black" text="white">

<TABLE bgColor = "black" border = "10" bordercolorlight = "white" bordercolordark =
"#554644" width = "100%" height = "23%">
<TR>
<TD width = "10%" bgColor = "black" ><FONT COLOR = "yellow"> Your graphics
goes here </FONT></TD>
<TD width = "90%"  bgColor = "black" align = "center"><H1><HR color =
"red">Heading<HR color = "red"></H1></TD>
</TR>
</TABLE>

<TABLE border = "2" bordercolor = "red" bgColor = "black" width = "100%" height =
"3.5%">
<TR>
<TD width = "20%"> <center><B>Link 1</B></center></TD>
<TD width = "20%"> <center><B>Link 2</B></center></TD>
```

```
<TD width = "20%"> <center><B>Link 3</B></center></TD>
<TD width = "20%"> <center><B>Link 4</B></center></TD>
<TD width = "20%"> <center><B>Link 5</B></center></TD>
</TR>
</TABLE>
<P>
<B>The background image is not large enough to fit the whole screen and becomes tiled
four times.  This produces the effect of having four distinctively colored boxes on the
screen</B>
</P>
</TABLE>
</BODY>
</HTML>
```

Most of the code should already be familiar to you except two attributes which have been used for the first time.   You will have noticed that there were two attributes specifying the color of the border for the table instead of just bordercolor. These attributes are discussed below.

bordercolorlight and bordercolordark → These two attributes can be used to make the border of the table multicolored. This can give a 3-D effect on the person. There value can be specified as RGB or using normal English (i.e. white, red, etc.).

That concludes our session on tables. In order to get a feel of tables, you must experiment with them extensively. I would suggest trying to set up tables with different borders backgrounds, content and sizes before you go onto the next section. If you are stuck and don't understand what tables you should try out. Create the following tables:

- Create a table with two rows and two columns (a 2 by 2 table).
- Create a 3 by 3, 4 by 4, 2 by 1, and 5 by 3 table.

This was a very short primer on tables. You can learn more about tables from more advanced tutorials such as:

http://www.htmlgoodies.com/tutors/tbl.html
www.w3schools.com/html/html_tables.asp

This chapter is all about forms. Forms are used when you want feedback from users. Forms can get a bit complicated in places and are considered to be somewhat advanced HTML. For this reason, this section is not very detailed and merely teaches the basics of forms.

A form is initiated using the <FORM> tag. This will basically tell the browser that a form has been initiated and the fields that follow are the form elements. A form must be ended with an end tag (i.e. </FORM>).

The most common tag when using forms is the <input> tag. This tag is used to specify the name, type and value of the input.

Inserting a text input field into a form

Type in the following code in a Notepad file and save the file as "textboxf.html"

```
<HTML>
<HEAD>
<TITLE>
Form text box
</TITLE>
</HEAD>
<BODY>
<FORM>
Text Field 1 <INPUT TYPE = "TEXT" VALUE = "" NAME = "1">
<BR>
Text Field 2 <INPUT TYPE = "TEXT" VALUE = "" NAME = "2">
</FORM>
</BODY>
</HTML>
```

When viewed in a browser, your webpage should look similar to Figure f1

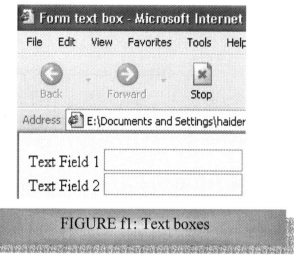

FIGURE f1: Text boxes

Let's break down the new commands:

> This is the label for the text box. It is typed outside the input tag. Same principle behind checkboxes and radio buttons

Text Field 1 <INPUT TYPE = "TEXT" VALUE = "" NAME = "1">

TYPE tells the browser what the form element will be, i.e. text box, checkbox, radio button...

VALUE tells the browser what the default value for the element is. In this case there is no default value so there is no text within the inverted commas.

NAME gives the element a specific name. This can be used to reference the element. For example: for creating a link which takes the person to the element.

NOTE: The NAME and VALUE attributes are not required. If these were not included, the webpage would still appear the same in this case.

Inserting a text area

If you want a larger area for the user to type comments in, you have to use the <textarea>. This tag allows you to specify how many rows and columns you want your text area to be. This is particularly useful for taking user comments.

Below is an example of the textarea tag. Type in the code into Notepad and name the file "textarea.html".

```
<HTML>
<HEAD>
<TITLE>
Textarea
</TITLE>
</HEAD>
<BODY>
<FORM>
```

```
<TEXTAREA NAME = "choice" ROWS = "5" COLS = "30">
</TEXTAREA>
</FORM>
</BODY>
</HTML>
```

You should see the screen shown in Figure f2 when you view the file in a browser

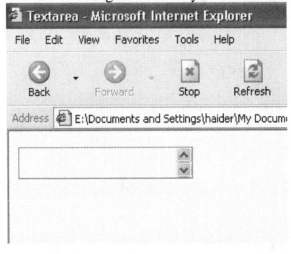

FIGURE f2: Textarea

Inserting Checkboxes

Type in the following code into Notepad and save the file as "checkbox.html"

```
<HTML>
<HEAD>
<TITLE>
Checkboxes
</TITLE>
</HEAD>
<BODY>
<FORM>
Who invented HTML?<BR>
<INPUT TYPE = "CHECKBOX" VALUE = "Bill Gates" NAME = "choice1"> Bill
Gates<BR>
<INPUT TYPE = "CHECKBOX" VALUE = "Tom Hanks" NAME = "choice2"> Tom
Hanks <BR>
<INPUT TYPE = "CHECKBOX" VALUE = "Tim Berners Lee" NAME = "choice3">
Tim Berners Lee <BR>
</FORM>
</BODY>
</HTML>
```

When viewed in a browser, you should see the screen shown in f3

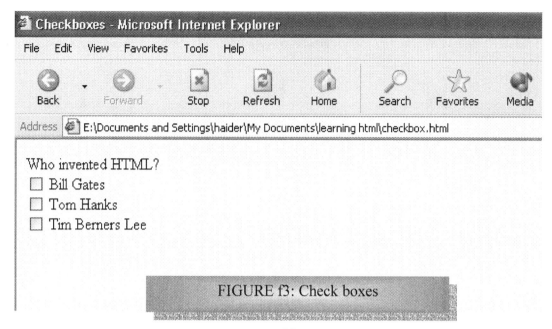

FIGURE f3: Check boxes

Clicking on the checkboxes should tick them ☑.

Let's look at the code for the checkbox in further detail.

> This is the text on the right of the checkbox, i.e. the label of the checkbox

<INPUT TYPE = "CHECKBOX" VALUE = "Bill Gates" NAME = "choice1"> Bill Gates

TYPE = "CHECKBOX" indicates to the browser that the element is a checkbox.
VALUE: This is the value of the checkbox. Note that this is NOT the text that is displayed to the right of the text box. This is basically for reference purposes.
NAME is the name of the checkbox. The name has to be decided on by the user. It is basically useful when the element is linked to or referred to for some other reason.

NOTE: Once again, the VALUE and NAME attributes are not mandatory. Merely specifying the type would still produce the same screen as shown in Figure f2.

If you want the checkbox to already be checked when page loads, all you have to do is type CHECKED in coding. E.g. for the last example, if we wanted Bill Gates to already be checked, we would type in the following:.

<INPUT **CHECKED** TYPE = "CHECKBOX" VALUE = "Bill Gates" NAME = "choice1"> Bill Gates

Inserting Radio buttons

Type the following into Notepad and save the file as "radio buttons.html"

```
<HTML>
<HEAD>
<TITLE>
Radio buttons
</TITLE>
</HEAD>
<BODY>
<FORM>
What is your favourite sport? <BR>
<INPUT TYPE = "RADIO" VALUE = "cricket" NAME = "choice"> Cricket <BR>
<INPUT TYPE = "RADIO" VALUE = "football" NAME = "choice"> Football <BR>
<INPUT TYPE = "RADIO" VALUE = "rugby" NAME = "choice"> Rugby <BR>
</FORM>
</BODY>
</HTML>
```

NOTE: All three radio buttons have been named "choice". This ensures that only one of the three choices can be selected at a time and there are no multiple selections. i.e. you cannot choose both cricket and football as your favourite games. You can only choose one. Having different names would mean that the user could check all three of the radio buttons at the same time.

When you view this file in a browser, you should see the screen shown in Figure f4

FIGURE f4: Radio Buttons

91

Inserting a button

Inserting buttons into a webpage also makes use of the <INPUT> tag. The type of input in this case is "button" as you may have guessed.

Type in the following into Notepad and save the file as "button.html"

```
<HTML>
<HEAD>
<TITLE>
Buttons
</TITLE>
</HEAD>
<BODY>
<FORM>
<INPUT TYPE = "BUTTON" VALUE = "test">
</FORM>
</BODY>
</HTML>
```

You should see the screen shown in Figure f5 when you view the file in a browser.

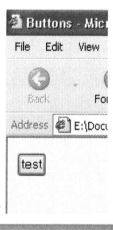

FIGURE f5: A Button

As you will have noticed, clicking the button does not do anything. The button has no function. We need to specify what will happen when we click it. This is done using a bit of simple **JavaScript**. We could set up the button to take us to a different website upon clicking it. In order to do this, a new attribute will be added to the <input> tag. This attribute will be as follows:

onClick = "window.location = 'www.hotmail.com'"

The onClick is a **JavaScript** command. It tells the browser what to do when something is clicked. In this case, it tells the browser what to do when the button is clicked. The command enclosed in the quotation marks after the equal sign is what the browser will do when the button is clicked. In this case we have told the browser to go to www.hotmail.com. The **window.location** is also **JavaScript**. "window" is called an object. The details of this are beyond the scope of this book. Basically, window.location tells the browser to change the current page opened in that window to the one specified after the equals sign.

Note that the website was specified within single quotation marks and not double ones. This is due to the fact that double quotation marks were used for enclosing window.location. i.e. "window.location = "www.hotmail.com"" would not be considered as good coding since the browser may get confused as to where each quotation mark terminates.

The code for the new button would now be as follows: (NOTE: I have changed the value of the button to "Go to Hotmail" since it makes more sense to name it that)

```
<HTML>
<HEAD>
<TITLE>
Button Redirection
</TITLE>
</HEAD>
<BODY>
<FORM>
<INPUT TYPE = "BUTTON" VALUE = "Go to Hotmail" onClick = "window.location
= 'www.hotmail.com' ">
</FORM>
</BODY>
</HTML>
```

You should see the screen shown in Figure f6 when you view the file in a browser. Clicking the button should now take you to www.hotmail.com

FIGURE f6: Button Redirection

Creating a Reset Button

Forms on the Internet occasionally have a **reset** button which when clicked clears all of the fields in the form. i.e. it empties all text fields, unselects all checkboxes....

Creating a reset button is very simple. Once again, the <input> tag is used. This time the type is specified as **reset**. That's it! The button will now reset the form.

An example of a form with a reset button is given below. Type in the code into Notepad and save the file as "reset button.html".

```
<HTML>
<HEAD>
<TITLE>
Reset Button
</TITLE>
</HEAD>
<BODY>
<FORM>
text box 1 <INPUT TYPE = "TEXT"> <BR>
Checkbox 1 <INPUT TYPE = "checkbox"> <BR>
Radio button 1 <INPUT TYPE = "radio" NAME = "choice"> <BR>
<INPUT TYPE = "reset">
</FORM>
</BODY>
</HTML>
```

Figure f7 illustrates what you should see once you open the page within a browser.

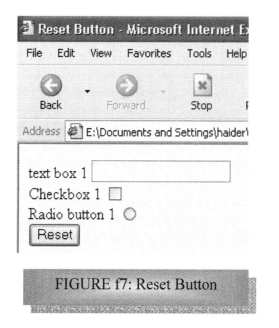

FIGURE f7: Reset Button

After you open the page, type something in the text box and select the checkbox and radio button. Then click the reset button. The text box should now become blank and the checkbox and radio button should become unchecked. You should note that the VALUE attribute was not included for the reset button. The browser will name the button "Reset" if a value is not specified. However, if you wish to have a different name, you may include the VALUE attribute and specify your desired name.

Creating a drop-down list

A drop-down list does not make use of the <input> tag. The code used for a drop-down list is as follows:

```
<SELECT NAME = "choose">
<OPTION VALUE = "choice 1"> Choice 1
<OPTION VALUE = "choice 2"> Choice 2
<OPTION VALUE = "choice 3"> Choice 3
</SELECT>
```

The code is quite self-explanatory. The <select> tag starts off the drop-down list. The name attribute specifies the name for the drop-down list. The <option> tags represent the different choices the drop-down list will contain.

The following is a sample webpage. Type the code into Notepad and save the file as "dropdownlist.html":

```
<HTML>
<HEAD>
<TITLE>
Drop-down lists
</TITLE>
</HEAD>
<BODY>
<FORM>
<SELECT NAME = "choose">
<OPTION VALUE = "choice 1"> Choice 1
<OPTION VALUE = "choice 2"> Choice 2
<OPTION VALUE = "choice 3"> Choice 3
</SELECT>
</FORM>
</BODY>
</HTML>
```

Open the file in a browser. You should see the screen shown in Figure f8. Clicking on the small arrow on the side should enable the list to pop down and you can now select one of the options.

95

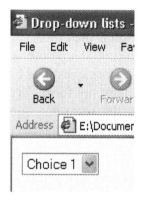

FIGURE f8: Drop-down list

Submitting a form

Although creating a submit button is very simple and merely requires the **type** in the <input> tag to be specified as submit, the actual submission, i.e. specifying where to submit to and what to submit is somewhat complicated. Unfortunately, this is beyond the scope of this book as it is CGI scripting and the main purpose of this book is to get the reader acquainted with basic HTML first.

One method of using HTML for form submission that can be used is as follows (however, it may not work in some browsers):

In the <form> tag, add two more attributes as follows:

<FORM method = "post" action = "mailto:examplemail@emailhost.com">

This is a very unreliable method of form submission. DO NOT use this for any important feedback since it may not work on every machine. You should merely use this method to test and see what the submitted form will look like.

If you want a real submission system, you would either have to learn CGI script in order to set up your own form submission or you could take the easy way out and go to www.response-o-matic.com. They provide a free service whereby you don't have to do any coding and they will set up the CGI script for you!

EXERCISE 6:

1) Create a form which uses text fields to collect personal information about people (name, address telephone...).
2) To this form, add the following:
   a. A question which asks the user to tick his favourite football team from the list. Use checkboxes to create the list which should contain at least 4 entries.
   b. A question which asks the user to select his gender from the two choices. Use radio-buttons.

c. A question which asks the user his current occupation. Create a drop-down list with common professions.

3) Improve your form by splitting it up into a personal section and a questions section. Be creative and add more questions on your own.

4) Add a reset and submit button to the form. Set it up so that the form is emailed to your e-mail address. Fill in the form and submit it to your account to see if it works and to see what a form looks like when it is emailed to you.

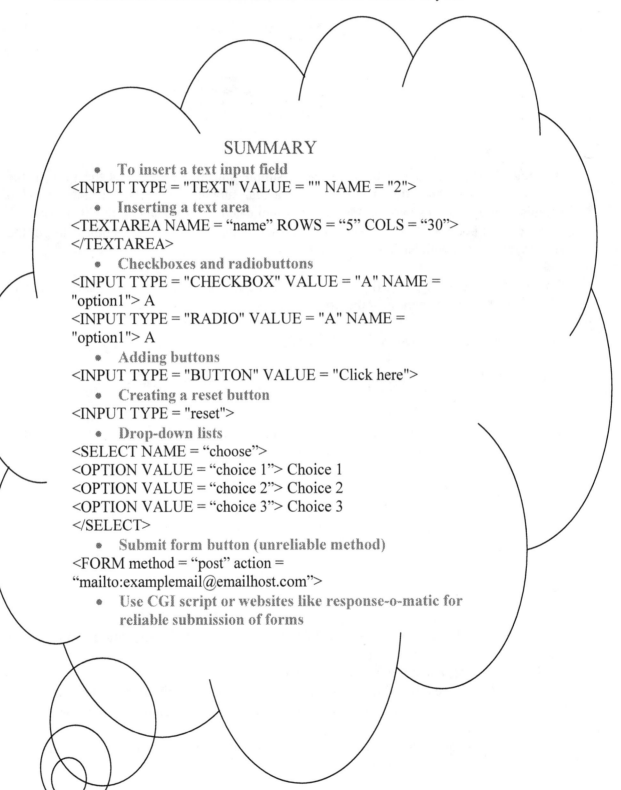

SUMMARY

- **To insert a text input field**

`<INPUT TYPE = "TEXT" VALUE = "" NAME = "2">`

- **Inserting a text area**

`<TEXTAREA NAME = "name" ROWS = "5" COLS = "30"> </TEXTAREA>`

- **Checkboxes and radiobuttons**

`<INPUT TYPE = "CHECKBOX" VALUE = "A" NAME = "option1"> A`
`<INPUT TYPE = "RADIO" VALUE = "A" NAME = "option1"> A`

- **Adding buttons**

`<INPUT TYPE = "BUTTON" VALUE = "Click here">`

- **Creating a reset button**

`<INPUT TYPE = "reset">`

- **Drop-down lists**

`<SELECT NAME = "choose">`
`<OPTION VALUE = "choice 1"> Choice 1`
`<OPTION VALUE = "choice 2"> Choice 2`
`<OPTION VALUE = "choice 3"> Choice 3`
`</SELECT>`

- **Submit form button (unreliable method)**

`<FORM method = "post" action = "mailto:examplemail@emailhost.com">`

- **Use CGI script or websites like response-o-matic for reliable submission of forms**

How to publish your website

Once you have made your website, you have to upload it onto the World Wide Web. If you have never done this before it can be quite confusing if you don't have someone to tell you what is going on. However, you have nothing to worry about as I will soon explain the concept of **web hosting** to you.

The websites you see on the Internet are all **hosted** by a **server**. The **server** can be defined as being a powerful computer which saves all the websites that you want to put on the Internet. The difference between your computer and the server is that the server is connected to the Internet 24 hours a day and 7 days a week (it is obviously disconnected sometimes for maintenance purposes, etc). The reason you need a server is so that other people can view your webpage even when you are not connected to the Internet.

The **Internet** is merely a network of computers spread all over the world. There is no central place where all of the computers link together. For someone to be part of this network, he or she must be connected to the Internet. Therefore, if someone wanted to view your website when you were offline, it would not be possible because the webpage files are not available. This is why a server is used. The server keeps a copy of the webpage files and even when you are **not** online, people can access your website because the files for the website are being provided by the server and *not* you.

Now the question arises, where can I find a server to **host** my website?

Finding a server

The company that hosts your website is called your **web host**. There are *many* web hosts; some are *free* while others cost money. There is always a catch to the free web hosts though. They usually place advertisements on your webpage in exchange for free hosting. Some of them don't place any advertisements *but* the **domain name** that free web hosts provide are very lengthy and are **not** like 'www.mysitename.com' or 'www.mysitename.org'. The domain names free web hosts provide are usually of the form www.companysname.com/members/~mysitename. Some free hosts place both advertisements and only provide very lengthy domains. The advertisements are placed either on your webpage or are in the form of pop-ups.

If you are looking to make a webpage which is merely for testing or is not that important, using a free web host is better than wasting money to purchase web space. If, **however,** you own a company and are making the company's website, it is *strongly recommended* that you buy a website rather than use free web hosts. When you buy a website, make sure you ask how much web space they provide. There is a limit as to the amount of files you can upload to the server. The limit is set by the web hosts, for example, the limit can be 50 MB, in which case the net size of all your webpage files should not exceed this value.

Now the question still remains: Where can I find a **web host** for my website.

Fortunately, there is a very good website called http://www.freewebspace.net that serves as a **web host search engine**. You can even specify what type of web host you are looking for (i.e. how much web space you want, should there be ads, etc).

There is also another website www.fateback.com. This website allows you to choose from a range of **domain names**. One reason I like this website is because the domains are quite short. For example: www.mysite.**yoll.net**

One last site I would recommend due to its mere popularity is yahoo. Yes, www.yahoo.com. Yahoo also provides free web hosting services. If you want to use yahoo's web hosting, then go to yahoo website and look for its web hosting service. The link to your website will, however, be quite long.

For example: www.geocities.com/....... (Yahoo geocities is the name of yahoo's web hosting service).

Yahoo also places advertisements on the webpage. This is why I am not particularly fond of yahoo's web hosting service.

What are you waiting for? Go online and find yourself a decent web host which fits your requirements!

Found a host, how do I get my files on it?

Register your account with the web host and write down the username and password (in case you forget). After you create your account, use the **username** and **password** to log into the account that you have just created. Look for the file manager. Open it and start uploading files onto the server. Note that there is usually an "**index.html**" file already on the server; you must replace this file with the file that you want as your website's home page. Remember that the page that you want to appear when someone accesses your website (i.e. your main page) must be called "**index.html**". If it is called for example: "first.html", the user will have to type in www.sitename.com/**first**. If he just types www.sitename.com, the website will not work since the browser does not know what page is the main page. After uploading the desired web page files log out and preview your web page. Note that if you have placed images or music on your website, they must also be uploaded onto the web host's server.

If you have visited www.freewebspace.net and browsed the website a bit, you will have come across **FTP support** in the description of some web hosts. **FTP** is the abbreviation for **File Transfer Protocol**. You can use an **FTP program** to upload files to a server as well. This way you don't have to go to your web hosts website and can just open the FTP program, connect to the Internet and type in the username and password to log in and start uploading files. Some people prefer **FTP programs** rather than having to go to the website every time, logging in and having to go to the file manager. **FTP programs** are available online for download; some are free while others have to be bought. One of the free FTP programs is **FTP Explorer** and if you want shareware, you can download **CuteFTP**. If you want to use an FTP program, you will need your web hosts ftp address. If you don't have it, email the technical support personnel of your web host. First, make sure you check your email after registering the account with the web host. They usually email you the details of your account, the ftp address along with other relevant information.

NOTE: NOT ALL WEB HOSTS SUPPORT FTP.

So, now the question changes to: where do I find an FTP program.

There are many FTP programs on the web, two of which are "CuteFTP Pro" and "BulletProof FTP".

You can also search the web for other FTP programs. After you have downloaded your desired FTP program, open it and connect to the Internet. Type in the ftp address of your web host and type in the username and password for your web host account. Then connect to the website. Upload the webpage files from your computer onto the web hosts' server. After you finish, type in your websites **URL** into the **browser** to see your website in action.

Note that sometimes it may take 24 hours or even longer before your website becomes updated with the new pages that you have uploaded. The time that elapses from when you uploaded the files to when the new version of the webpage appears online depends entirely on the web host you use.

Search Engines

Those of you who have already published their website and have tried searching for it in a search engine will probably have been surprised that they couldn't find their site.

So why is it that your website isn't listed on any search engine? Well, the reason is simple. You need to submit your website to the specific search engines. This can **sometimes** cost money. There are programs you can buy which will submit your website to several search engines (sometimes even to over a 100) but I *wouldn't* recommend them because you can't really be sure that the website has actually been submitted.

Fortunately, many search engines are still free. Below is a list of the popular search engines that are still free:

Google: (www.google.com) is one of the most widely used search engine and I personally prefer it. To submit your URL, go to http://www.google.com/webmasters/

Yahoo: (www.yahoo.com) is free for non-commercial websites only. (Fees required for commercial use). It is very popular and used by a vast majority of people.

DMOZ: The Open Directory Project: (http://www.dmoz.org) is also very important for submitting your websites to as search engines like google and many others draw their directories from here.

AllTheWeb: (http://www.alltheweb.com/)

Zeal: (http://www.zeal.com/)

MSN: (http://www.msn.com) For submission go to the following URL:
http://submitit.bcentral.com/msnsubmit.htm

AltaVista: (http://www.altavista.com/) For submissions go to
http://www.altavista.com/addurl/

HotBot: (http://www.hotbot.com/)

Alexa: (http://www.alexa.com/) To submit your site, go to
http://pages.alexa.com/help/webmasters/

NationalDirectory: (http://www.nationaldirectory.com/addurl/) To list your site, go to
http://www.nationaldirectory.com/addurl

whatUseek: (http://www.whatuseek.com) For submissions go to
http://www.whatuseek.com/addurl-secondary.shtml

NOTE: Directories are search engines which are powered by humans. That means that humans select and rate the sites in the search engine.

Meta tags

Some search engines make use of the meta tag when rating websites. Although this tag is not supported by some search engines, it is best to include it in your web pages. Let's look at how to use the meta tag in some detail.

The meta tag is always included in the head section of the webpage and must be entered in between the opening and closing <HEAD> tag. The two main meta tags worth mentioning are meta description tags and meta keyword tags.

Meta description tag

In the meta description tag, you include a brief description of what your website is about. This description is then used by some search engines as the description for your website in their search results. The description should be about 200 words in length. The following is an example of a meta description tag for a website. This description is a possible description for a website which teaches you HTML.

<HEAD>
<TITLE> A visual approach to HTML </TITLE>
<META NAME = "description" CONTENT = "This tutorial teaches you all there is to know about HTML. It is meant for beginners and was written by Haider Syed.">
</HEAD>

As you will have noticed, there is no end tag. The name attribute is used to specify the type of the meta tag. The content attribute contains the actual description.

Meta keywords tag

This tag allows you to enter a few keywords that when used by people would enable them to find your site. So in other words, these keywords are relevant to the content of your site and represent what your site is about. Although, this tag does not enjoy support from many crawler-based search engines, you should still include it. The tag might help boost your rating if you have specified a keyword which is also found frequently in the body of your webpage. Let's look at an example.

```
<HEAD>
<TITLE> A visual approach to HTML </TITLE>
<META NAME = " keywords" CONTENT = "html, learning html, html for beginners,
html for dummies">
</HEAD>
```

Once again, as you can see, the meta tag has been placed between the <HEAD> opening and closing tag. The type of tag is specified using the "name" attribute as before and the "content" attribute contains the keywords you want your site to be found for.

If we were to combine the meta keywords tag and the meta description tag for the examples we have just covered the code would look like this:

```
<HEAD>
<TITLE> A visual approach to HTML </TITLE>
<META NAME = "description" CONTENT = "This tutorial teaches you all there is to
know about HTML. It is meant for beginners and was written by Haider Syed.">
<META NAME = " keywords" CONTENT = "html, learning html, html for beginners,
html for dummies">
</HEAD>
```

Note that the <meta> tag does not have an end tag.

There are also other types of meta tags but these are the two main ones that should concern you for now.

Crawler-based search engines

Some search engines, including google, are crawler based. Crawler based search engines look for websites and they follow links on websites. If they think your website is worth it, they may even add your link to their search engine listing for free.

Getting listed with important directories such as DMOZ is crucial because you will stand a better chance of being found by crawler-based search engines and being listed by them for free.

Before you submit to a directory, make sure you write about a 20 word description of your site. This description should also contain a few keywords which when used by people would allow them to find your site with. So these keywords should be representative of your site's content.

Be sure to include the **Meta tag** in the source code of your website (inside the head tag). Only *some* search engines actually use it but you should include it anyway. (Google ignores the meta tag description you see in the search results. This description has generated by Google).

It is crucial that your website shows up in the first page of the search results. Research has shown that a majority of people don't even bother looking at the rest of the pages outputted by the search results.

Note that you don't have to submit your website to search engines. You will still get some traffic anyway. Your web host will most probably list your website in the appropriate category of their site so people can go to it. Obviously, this will only be minimal traffic and it is not something you should depend on for all your traffic. You can't expect to get your **intended** traffic through your web host's site.

Why would people pay if they can get their site listed for free?

With free submissions it is not guaranteed that your site will get listed and it also takes about a month even if they do accept. If you pay, however, it is usually faster than that depending on which search engine you are at. Some search engines even allow you to increase your rating in exchange for some money.

Search Engine Optimization

Search engine optimization means altering your page in ways that you will get a higher ranking with search engines for specific terms. Note that search engine optimization does **NOT** apply to open directories. The reason is that directories are dependant on humans. Humans are subjective and they can judge the relevancy quality of your page by looking at it.

There are quite a few ways of optimizing your page. However, I will only mention some of the main ones briefly. The search engine is not human-based and it will not look at your page the way a human would. As a result search engines have a set of rules to follow for ranking your page. If you use these rules to make your page decent for search engines, they will obviously rank you highly. The following are some of the ways that search engines use to rank your page.

The "**title**" tag is very important. The search engine will look at your keywords and compare them with the title of your page. The keywords (preferably the first two or three words that are the most important) should appear in the title of the page. The keywords that you have used should also appear in the first few paragraphs of your page (preferably more than once). The reason for this is that the search engine assumes if the topic is actually relevant, it will be mentioned right from the beginning.

Search engines cannot see pictures. If you fill your webpage with pictures, the search engine could rank you poorly since it will not see the relevance. Always use the "**Alt**" tag with all of your pictures. Some search engines will look at the alt tag but you should try to add some text next to the picture wherever possible.

Search engines use something called link analysis to rate your site. The search engine basically searches your site for other website links. These website links must not just be links to any sites, they have to be links to sites that relate to the topic that you have on your site. It is not really a matter of quantity but more a matter of quality. The sites that you provide links for should be popular for the keywords that you want your site to be located with. The way you find sites to link to is simple. Just go to search engines and search for the keywords you want to be relevant for your site. Go to the sites you find in the results and ask them if they will allow you to provide a link for them (and vice versa).

Making it accessible for search engines

Some search engines don't support frames or image maps. If you have image maps on your site, make sure that you also have html hyperlinks on the page that can be used to access the pages. Otherwise, the search engine may not even be able to get into your pages and so it might decide that your website is not worth indexing. Some of the chief search engines get stumbled by frames. They can't follow the frame links. There are some solutions to this but I would just suggest **NOT** using frames at all. There are lots of websites out there that just reprove of frames and don't like them. The reason is that they are not used efficiently sometimes. They can get annoying when things like a horizontal scrollbar appear and so on.

I would also suggest that you refrain from using symbols in your URLs as well since it gets in the way of some search engines.

Search Engine Spamming

In order to get a higher rating with search engines, some webmasters try to trick the browsers. Tricks include writing the keywords repeatedly on the side of the page in a very small font so that they are invisible. Some webmasters write the keywords in the same color as the background of the webpage. These are old tricks and most search engines are already accustomed to them. They will usually have appropriate software to detect such spamming. If they find that you are spamming, your site might even be banned from the search engine. My advice to you is, **"Don't even think about it"**.

Make sure that the sentences on your webpage are grammatically correct. You never know what methods search engines may devise to look for spamming.

What about when you update?

When you update your site, you should resubmit it to the search engine as some search engines only check for updates annually.

One last thing

A simple search engine is quite easy to program and can be done with some knowledge of ASP. Major search engines like Google, however, have very complex **algorithms**. What are algorithms you ask? The logic behind a program needs to be understood before the program is created. It is first represented as a diagram on paper which shows the flow of data in the program. In this case, saying that Google has a very complex algorithm means that the rules (or let's say logic) that it utilizes are very complex.

Google tries to understand how the human mind approaches the search engine and is programmed along those lines, so that it can cope with the diversity of searches made and still manage to bring back the most relevant links. Google enjoys popularity among the people mainly due to its user-friendly interface and quick, yet efficient search system which seldom fails to return relevant search results if used properly. The fact that there are no fancy animations also means that the page loads up very quickly. This is especially an attraction for advanced net users who are notorious for their impatience. Its easy to use interface also attracts the novice users and its advanced search options keep the advanced users happy as well. Google may seem like a simple website but in reality, there are thousands of people working in the background to maintain and improve its searching capabilities.

If you submit your website to Google and notice that your website is in the top 3 for a specific term and then suddenly moves down to the top 10, this would probably be due to the fact that Google is always changing its algorithm for ranking websites to make sure that it doesn't fall victim to search engine spamming and to ensure that the users get the most relevant search results.

SECTION B:
BONUS CHAPTERS

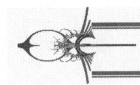 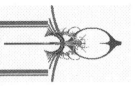

JavaScript is a very useful language if you want to make your website interactive. JavaScript is a separate language from HTML. It is a common mistake to assume that JavaScript is the same as the programming language JAVA; this is simply *not* true. JAVA is more complex than JavaScript and is harder to learn.

The best part about JavaScript is that you do not need any additional software to run it just like with HTML. As long as your browser supports JavaScript, all you need is Notepad to type in the code.

JavaScript can be used to do a number of things. Some of the tasks which can be accomplished are mouse roll-over effects, form validation, pop-ups, confirmation messages, alerts and prompts. JavaScript can be used for numerous other purposes ranging in complexity from creating calculators to displaying simple text on a web page.

In this book, I will only cover some very basic JavaScript so that you can add an element of interactivity to your web page.

The Basics

1. The browser needs to know that the code that you have entered is JavaScript code and not HTML. Therefore, you must differentiate the code from the rest of the document by encapsulating it within the <script> tag.

2. JavaScript code is case-sensitive. That means that capitals (upper-case) and lower-case are different from each other. Using the wrong letter-case can cause errors.

3. JavaScript commands end with a **semi-colon (;)**. (This is also common among programming languages like Pascal).

You don't have to memorize the above rules; it is advisable to keep them in mind. Now that you know some of the fundamentals of JavaScript, let's go ahead and learn some JavaScript code.

Writing text

You are about to write your first JavaScript code. It may not be very complex and it may not do much but it's a start. The code is very simple and merely displays text in the body of the web page. The use of this script may not seem very apparent at this moment but you will soon learn why you need to know how to include text on a web page using JavaScript versus doing just the same with HTML.

The code for the web page is given below. Most books and tutorials on computer languages will start off by creating the conventional Hello World! web page. Since I did not start off the HTML part of this book using that example, I decided to include it in the JavaScript section to continue the legacy!

Type in the following code into Notepad and save the file as "helloworld.html". (Note that even if though you are using JavaScript, the file extension will still be .html).

```
<HTML>
<HEAD>
<TITLE>
My JavaScript web page
</TITLE>
</HEAD>
<BODY>
<script language = "JavaScript">
document.write("Hello World!");
</script>
</BODY>
</HTML>
```

When you view the web page in the browser, you should see the screen shown in Figure b1

FIGURE b2: Using document.write

Let's look at the code in more detail:

<script language = "JavaScript"> → indicates to the browser that the code that follows is written in JavaScript.

document.write("Hello World!"); → this is the actual JavaScript code. **document.write** tells the browser to print onto the document the words that are enclosed within the parentheses and quotation marks. The **semi-colon (;)** must be inserted at the end of every command.

</script> → instructs the browser that the JavaScript code has ended.

Alerts

Most of you will have come across a JavaScript alert box at some point in time during your web experience. Ever thought of making one yourself? Alert boxes are very simple and easy to make. If you are not sure what an alert box is, Figure b2 gives an example.

FIGURE b2: A JavaScript alert box

Let's look at an example on alerts. Type in the following code into Notepad and save the file as alerts.html:

```
<HTML>
<HEAD>
<TITLE>
JavaScript Alerts
</TITLE>
</HEAD>
<BODY>
<script language = "JavaScript">
alert("Text enclosed between the inverted commas will appear in the alert box.");
</script>
</BODY>
</HTML>
```

If you typed in the code correctly, you should see the alert shown in Figure b3 appear when you open the web page in the browser.

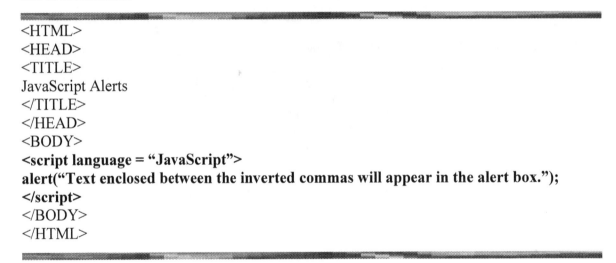

FIGURE b3: JavaScript alert box

Let's break down the code for the example web page:

<script language = "JavaScript"> → tells the browser that the code which follows is JavaScript. Note that, typing only **<script>** is also enough.

alert("Text enclosed between the inverted commas will appear in the alert box."); → is the actual JavaScript code (note another name for quotation marks is inverted commas). **alert** tells the browser to display an alert box, The brackets and the inverted commas enclose the text that will be displayed in the alert box. The **;** (semi-colon) that follows ends the command.

</script> → tells the browser that the JavaScript code has ended.

Some of you may think that this is a bit lengthy to commit to memory but with practice, it should become more straight-forward.

Make sure you memorize the layout for the alert statement. All you have to remember is that you have to type **alert** followed by parentheses and quotation marks, then type the text to be displayed in the alert box and close the quotation marks and parentheses. Make sure you end the line with a semi-colon (;).

Variables

Variables are data stores. They can be thought of as boxes which can store information. In order to keep track of all the variables (boxes), they are given names. Therefore, variables are used to store information and each variable is given a name so that if it needs to be accessed later on, the variable can be called.

Variables can be quite useful. For example, you could ask a person to input his name and store the name in a variable and then later on use it to print his name on the web page.

The data that variables contain is *not* fixed which means that the data can be changed. They are known as **variables** since their value can *vary*.

Read on to find out how you can use variables.

Confirmation boxes

Confirmation boxes are dialog boxes which basically ask the user a question, the user either clicks Ok or Cancel in response to the question. The choice the person makes is stored in a "variable". Let's look at an example:

```
<HTML>
<HEAD>
<TITLE>
Confirmation boxes
</TITLE>
<script>
var response
```

```
</script>
</HEAD>
<BODY>
<script>
response=confirm("Jump to hotmail");
if (response)
window.location="http://www.hotmail.com"
</script>
</BODY>
</HTML>
```

You should see the confirmation box shown in Figure b4 when you view the webpage in the browser.

FIGURE b3: A confirmation box

Lets' break down the code:

var response → This introduces the variable.

response=confirm("Jump to hotmail"); → This assigns the variable the value of the response of the confirmation box.

if (response)
window.location="http://www.hotmail.com" → This tells the browser that if the response is ok, then the hotmail website should open in the same window.

Prompts

Prompts are basically dialog boxes which appear asking the user for information such as his name. The information can then be stored in a variable and used later. An example of a web page which uses variables is shown below:

```
<HTML>
<HEAD>
<TITLE>
Haider's webpage
</TITLE>
<script language = "Javascript">
var password;
```

```
var pass;
var pass="html";
password=prompt('Please enter the provided password!',' ');
if (password==pass)
alert('Password has been accepted! You are authorised to access this page!');
else
{
window.location="www.unauthorised.html";
}
</SCRIPT>
</HEAD>
<BODY>
<script language="Javascript">
var yourname=prompt('Please type your name and press enter',' ');
if ( (yourname== ' ') || (yourname==null) )
{
yourname="Man";
}
</script>
<P>
<script language = "Javascript">
document.write("<CENTER><h1>Hey, " + yourname + "! Welcome to my
webpage! </h1></CENTER>");
</script>
</BODY>
</HTML>
```

Let's break down the JavaScript in this code:

<script language = "JavaScript"> → indicates to the browser that the code that follows is written in JavaScript.

var password; → introduces the variable password

var pass; → introduces the variable pass

var pass="html"; → assigns the value "html" to the variable pass
password = prompt('Please enter the provided password!',' '); → Prompts the user to enter the password and stores the value input as the value for the variable password.

if (password==pass)
alert('Password has been accepted! You are authorised to access this page!');
 → If the value stored in the variable password is equal to the value stored in the variable pass, the browser alerts the user "**Password has been accepted! You are authorised to access this page!**"

Note: The == is used in JavaScript to check if two values are equivalent to each other. Note that there are two equal signs and not one

112

else
{
window.location="www.unauthorised.html";
}

→ If the requirement for the "IF statement" is not true then the browser carries out the commands that are in the else statement. In this case, it redirects the browser to the webpage "www.unauthorised.html"

</script> → tells the browser that the JavaScript code has ended.

<script language="Javascript"> → Once again instructs the browser that the code that follows is JavaScript code.

var yourname=prompt('Please type your name and press enter',' '); → Prompts the user for his/her name and stores the users response in the variable "yourname".

if (yourname== ' ')
{
yourname="Man";
}

→ If the user inputs a blank space as his name, the browser assigns the value of "Man" to the variable "yourname".

</script> → Once again, this tells the browser that the JavaScript code has ended.

<script language = "Javascript"> → This initiates another cluster of JavaScript code

document.write("<CENTER><h1>Hey, " + yourname + "! Welcome to my webpage! </h1></CENTER>"); → This tells the browser to write "Hey" in the body of the webpage followed by the value of the variable yourname (which is the name the person has entered.) which is followed by the words " ! Welcome to my webpage!"

</script > → Ends the JavaScript code once again.

If you type in the code into Notepad and view it in a browser, you should first see the prompt shown in Figure b4.

FIGURE b4: Internet Explorer prompt

113

On typing in the correct password (in this case "html") and clicking OK, you should see the alert shown in Figure b5

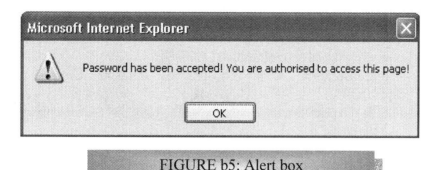

FIGURE b5: Alert box

After clicking OK again, the prompt shown in Figure b6 should now appear

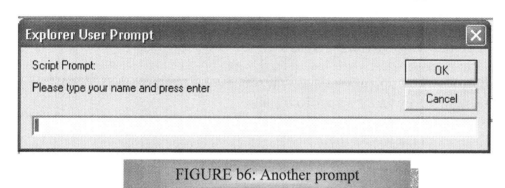

FIGURE b6: Another prompt

Once you enter your name and click OK, the webpage should now say "Hey, Haider! Welcome to my webpage!" (Obviously with the name you entered instead of Haider)

IMPORTANT NOTE: Do not use the method outlined above for password protection. Old browsers do not support JavaScript and will merely ignore the JavaScript code and therefore the users will not have to type in a password in order to access your webpage. The only reason password protection using JavaScript was shown was to illustrate to the reader how to use variables.

Some Further Examples:

This section contains two webpage examples.

1. **Form validation**

```
<HTML>
<HEAD>
<TITLE>Haider's Car Company</TITLE>
</HEAD>
<BODY>
<FORM NAME="form1">
<FIELDSET>
<LEGEND>Personal information</LEGEND>
```

```
Name    <INPUT TYPE="text" NAME="id"><BR>
Gender <INPUT TYPE="text" NAME="sex">
</FIELDSET><P>
</FORM>
<FIELDSET>
<LEGEND>When will you be dropping by</LEGEND>
Date              <INPUT TYPE="text" NAME="date"><BR>
<ACRONYM TITLE="Approximate">Approx.</ACRONYM>Time <INPUT
TYPE="text" NAME="time">
</FIELDSET><P>
</FORM>
<FORM NAME="form">
<FIELDSET>
<LEGEND>What type of car are you planning on buying</LEGEND>
Manufacturer <INPUT TYPE="text" NAME="manufacturer"><BR>
Model           
<INPUT TYPE="text" NAME="model">
</FIELDSET><BR>
<BUTTON NAME="submit" onClick="if (document.form.manufacturer.value=='')
alert('Manufacturer name is required'); else
{
alert('Thank you for your submission')
window.location='thankupage.html'
} ">Submit</button>
</FORM>
</HTML>
```

2. Password protection without using prompts

```
<HTML>
<HEAD>
<TITLE>
Password protection without using prompts
</TITLE>
</HEAD>
<script language = "JavaScript">
var password;
var pass1="html";
</script>
<BODY>
<FORM>
<TABLE BORDER="0" ALIGN="CENTER" CELLSPACING="0">
<TR>
<TD>USERNAME :</TD>
<TD><INPUT NAME="text" TYPE="text"><TD>
</TR>
<TR>
<TD>PASSWORD :</TD>
```

```html
<TD><INPUT NAME="text1" TYPE="password"></TD>
</TR>
<TR>
<TD> </TD>
<TD ALIGN="center">
<INPUT NAME="button" TYPE="button" value="log in" onClick=
"if (pass1 == form.text1.value)
{
alert('Password has been accepted! You are authorised to access this page!')
window.location='authorised.html'
}
else
{
alert('You typed in the wrong password.  Please try again.');
}">
</TD>
</TR>
</TABLE>
</FORM>
</BODY>
</HTML>
```

This chapter contains a number of tips and advice which should prove quite useful to you.

What shouldn't you do?

With the advent of time, the Internet has become a commonplace technology. The web is now full of content and information. There are billions of websites hosted by a variety of people for diverse reasons. In order to achieve high traffic to your site, you must do your best to attract and maintain the user's attention. Some people have misinterpreted this statement and have ended up losing potential traffic. The methods you apply for maintaining and attracting the user's attention should not be methods that will "**irritate**" the user. Some web masters think that using cool animations and fancy backgrounds is the best way to keep the user interested. This methodology, however, is extremely flawed. Although these elements may appeal to the inexperienced, it is not going to be such a treat for the advanced users. The reasoning is simple:

"Animations and images take time to load and for people with slow connections (and therefore slow download speeds), this can be a nightmare."

The above is not to suggest that you should simply make your webpage a white screen with some text on it. Rather, you should just stick with a colored background and a few animations (if you deem it necessary). Advanced users know the power of the web and they know that they can easily go to a search engine and find the same thing that you have to offer. The difference being that the other websites will probably not take as much time to load.

I would always recommend you to upload the website to the Internet and go to it to see how much time it takes to load. Obviously, this time will be different and will depend on the type and quality of the user's Internet connection. However, you can still make an educated guess about whether or not your site your site is loading fast enough. One way is to look at the file size of the images and videos, etc. If there are any files that are beyond 1 mega byte, it is obvious that your site will take a long time to load for some users.

As a general rule, if your site is taking time loading on a DSL connection, it requires serious attention because DSL is generally quite fast and it should only take a few seconds for your site to load. If the website takes a few minutes to load on a dial-up, you should try to minimize the loading time further.

A good site, in my opinion, is one that doesn't take more than half a minute to load on a 56K dial-up connection. It is worth noting that after a user has visited your website once, it should generally take less time for it to load on the next visit. Although with the advent of broadband Internet connections, the time it takes to load up a webpage is quite miniscule for broadband subscribers, one has to remember that in several locations around the world broadband is not that widespread yet, so keeping that mind is important.

The dreaded 'blink' and 'marquee' command

Using the blink command to attract attention is the equivalent of committing the ultimate sin. Imagine you are on a website and reading some text and there is some text on the side of the screen which keeps flashing every other second. You will notice that it will be extremely distracting and it will not be easy to concentrate. Your eyes will keep trying to focus on that side of the screen where the flashing text is located.

The marquee command is just as bad as the blink command. Let alone the distraction issue, think of what it does to the slow readers especially if the text string is long. The person will have to wait until the whole text string repeats itself if he for example, missed out some of it because he was reading too slowly.

Frames

Frames are quite notorious on the World Wide Web. The idea of being able to divide the page into different sections can help in creating a navigation system and seems at first to be quite a helpful tool. However, frames are widely disliked; the reason being that sometimes there misuse can lead to certain complications. Some browsers don't even support frames while at other times the problem is that the length of the text cannot fit into the specified area and so a small horizontal scrollbar has to be utilized to see the rest of the text. This is something that a majority of users tend to find extremely frustrating. One other thing about frames is that they can also sometimes cause problems for search engines when it comes to indexing your webpage.

Under Construction page

Web users have now become restless; studies show that users merely skim read web pages. For this reason, you have to be succinct and stick to the point. Sometimes, people haven't yet made a webpage and they place an "Under Construction" animated GIF on their page and ask users to check back soon. Using this method only merely infuriates the user for wasting his time for opening a page that has nothing on it. It is highly unlikely that he will bookmark your page and come back to it later. The key is merely to post your website **after** you have created it. Don't misinterpret this, if you have a webpage which has at least some content on it while some sections are still under construction, then by all means, post your website. However, if you have only the homepage done then you should have some patience and publish it online only after completing some other sections first.

For those of you who have some sections to build, I would recommend that using some JavaScript you set up a system where clicking on the link to the incomplete sections displays an **alert** stating "Under Construction..." Despite the fact that this may seem a bit low tech, it will save the user time as he will not have to wait for another page to open with the statement "Under Construction" displayed on it.

Background color and text

The contrast between your background color and the color of the text is an important issue to consider when designing webpages. The background color of your webpage and the color of the text must be distinctive so as to make the text more legible. Use your logic: Don't have a black background and put black text on it. The user won't even see the text. If you have a dark background, use a light color for the text. One of my personal favourites is white text on a black background. It even gives the page a hint of a professional look. Some of you will obviously want to use some other background colors like violet for example and might be wondering how you could find out the best suited text color. There is a very simple way of doing this. Open Microsoft paint. Click on the "Fill in color" button (the ink bottle with some black ink coming out of it). Choose the color that you want for the webpage's background and click on the white space. The white space should now be colored with the color that you specified. Now click on Image from the top menu bar and choose "Invert Colors". (You can also hold down Ctrl and press the letter "I"). The color should now be changed to what can be referred to as the opposite color. This is the color that you should use to make your text more readable.

Background images

Some of you may have dark background images and the text color might be white. Remember that the website takes time to load and therefore while the image is loading, the user will see a 'white' background and won't see the 'white' text on it. The user will probably think that there is nothing on the website and will leave before the background image loads. There is a very simple solution to this. Consider the following example. The background image is called 'darkforest', it is a bitmap file and the text color is white. The body tag should look as follows:

<BODY BACKGROUND = "darkforest.bmp" bgColor = "**black**" TEXT = "white">

This is why while the image is loading, the background color will appear black and therefore the user will be able to read your text even while the background image is loading.

Never Ending Page

Some webmasters put all their text on one page to avoid having to go through the hassle of making separate pages and linking them all together. This is a very bad way to do it. It makes it harder for the user to find what they are looking for and it is also very difficult to scroll through the text. Undoubtedly, this method is not a good way to attract traffic.

Business website

If your website is for a company or for a business, special consideration has to be taken. In this case, it especially becomes important to create a website that is both aesthetically pleasing as well as practical. You must make certain that there are no spelling mistakes or HTML coding errors as this will put a bad impression on your clientele. Your site must look impressive and preferably load quickly. If you do choose to have background music, make sure to make it appropriate for the site.

This chapter outlines various tricks which you can use in your web pages.

Bookmark link

This method only works for Microsoft's Internet Explorer web browser.

<a href = "javascript:window.external.AddFavorite('http://www.siteurl.com', 'Name under which you want to bookmark the link')"> Click this link to bookmark </a>

Changing background color for form fields

This code can be used to change the background color for text fields, drop-down menus, etc.

```
<form>
<input type = "text" name = "text field" style = "background-color:blue;">
</form>
```

Using images for form fields

This code allows you to use an image as the background for text fields, drop-down menus, etc.

```
<form>
<input type="text" name="name" style = "background-image:url('imagename.ext')">
</form>
```

Changing the color of a scroll-bar

The scroll bar can be divided into different sections and the color of each part can then be defined individually. Just type in the code below and change the values of the different colors and experiment. Each color represents a different section of the scrollbar. With some testing, you should be able to deduce for yourself which part each of the colors in the code represents. Note that some browsers do not support this tag. These browsers will just ignore the code as "<!--" has been used which represents a comment. Therefore, older browsers would just think that it is merely a comment.

This is an example of the use of CSS. CSS is discussed in more detail in the FAQ section.

```
<style type = "text/css">
<!--
Body {
scrollbar-face-color: #112233;
scrollbar-highlight-color:#abcdef;
```

```
scrollbar-3dlight-color:#119941;
scrollbar-darkshadow-color:blue;
scrollbar-shadow-color:yellow;
scrollbar-arrow-color:yellow;
scrollbar-track-color:#999999;
}
-->
  </style>
```

Adding effects to your pages when they open

When the page loads up, you can add several effects such as make it fade-in or have a circle from the middle enlarge until the whole page is visible. These effects are easy to code and can be achieved with DHTML. DHTML is *not* the same language as HTML, DHTML stands for Dynamic HTML. The code used to achieve these **page effects** is below. Include this code in the <head> area of your webpage.

```
<meta http-equiv="Page-Enter" content = "revealtrans(duration = 2.0 transition = 3)">
```

Changing the value of **"duration"** will change the time period for which the effect will occur and **"transition"** represents the number which in itself represents a specific effect. The value of transition can be from 0-23. Each number represents a predefined effect with the exception of 23. I would suggest that you try all the 24 numbers to see what each effect is. Note that 23 will produce a random page enter effect each time you enter the page.

To get a fade-in effect, you must use the following code:

```
<meta http-equiv="Page-Enter" content="blendtrans(duration=2.0)">
```

Note that it is the same code as above except that the content is **blendtrans** this time rather than **revealtrans** and there is *no* transition number. There is only *one* **blendtrans** (fade-in) effect which is why there is no transition number.

Last page modified

Some of you will have seen that many websites have a last updated or last modified date on them. This is something that can be easily included in your webpage too. Just type in the following source code wherever on the page you want the last modified date to appear.

```
<SCRIPT type="text/javascript">
<!--
document.write(document.lastModified);
//-->
</SCRIPT>
```

This code will merely write the date and time of modification. It will not create the sentence to go with the date; therefore you should write something like this:

```
<P Align = "center">This page was last updated on:
<SCRIPT type="text/javascript">
<!--
document.write(document.lastModified);
//-->
</SCRIPT></P>
```

Making a back button

Other than the conventional back button that is present on the browser, you can make your own back button. You can even specify how many pages back into the history it will take you.

```
<a href = "javascript:history.go(-1)"> Back to the previous page</a>
```

The **-1** takes the user back one page. If it was -3, it would take the user back 3 pages. You can use this to build a forward button too. Just remove the negative sign and it will change to a forward button. This page is based on the history list. It is merely a recreation of the browser's back button which will also still be functional even if you use this code to make another alternative back button.

Create a "Set to homepage" link

You can create a link on your webpage which when clicked will set the page as the homepage of the browser. Let's look at an example:

```
<HTML>
<HEAD>
<TITLE>
Set to homepage link
</TITLE>
</HEAD>
<BODY>
<A HREF = "#" onClick = "this.style.behavior = 'url (#default#homepage)';
this.setHomePage ('http://www.google.com');"> Click here to set this page as your
homepage</a>
</BODY>
</HTML>
```

When the link is clicked, the user will first see a confirmation box which will display: "Would you like to set your Home Page to "http://www.google.com"? If the user clicks "yes", the homepage will change to google.com.

Note that the link can be a text link, an image or even a button.

Quick Images

This trick is independent of the actual coding. Some of you will have noticed fonts like "Wingdings" and "Webdings" in Microsoft Word. Every letter that you type in outputs a picture. Try it! Open Microsoft Word and type in anything, then change the font to "Wingdings"; your text should now change into small images. Now change the font to "Webdings"; once again you will get a new set of images. Why not use these images in your websites! Some of them may not have any use but if you think intuitively you could probably use some images like the ones below:

The beauty of using these fonts for images is that since they are actually text, you won't even have to upload an image file. *However*, not everyone would have these fonts installed on their system so it would be best that if you wish to use these fonts, you should take a screen shot of the text and then paste it into a text editor (like Notepad) and then crop the image. This trick can help out if you're stuck and can't find the right image or if you just want to do things quickly.

If you increase the font size, the images don't loose their quality either since it is merely text. Look at the larger images below:

As you can see, these images appear quite well and with fine detail.

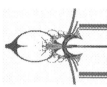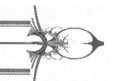

This chapter teaches you how to create logos and titles. Designing fancy logos or titles for a website can be difficult especially if you don't have the appropriate software. Software packages that deal with the creation of animated logos or 3D text can be quite expensive sometimes, not to mention that they can get a bit confusing too. For this reason, I decided to include a section on making titles/stationary logos using Microsoft Word. The reason I chose word is because it is quite popular and most computer users who use the computer for typing will already have it installed. Note that the method outlined for making logos/titles is not the professional way do it. There are programs as I mentioned earlier that have been specifically made for these purposes. This section is merely for those people who do not wish to spend money on such programs. All the logos in this section have been made by using Microsoft Word. Microsoft Paint was also used in some cases to a very minimal extent. I will use the following title as an example to teach you, step by step, the process of creating a title. Then I will give a few examples of titles along with some guidelines as to how they have been made. Some of the titles are fit to be used as logos.

INTRODUCTORY LEVEL JAVASCRIPT

Method: Create a text box by clicking on Insert in the MS Word menu at the top and select Text Box

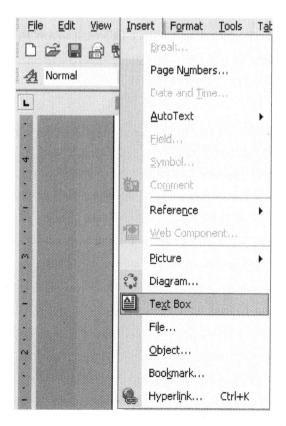

Drag the mouse cursor across the screen so as to create a text box that is approximately the same size as the text box shown below.

Right click the text box and select Add Text.

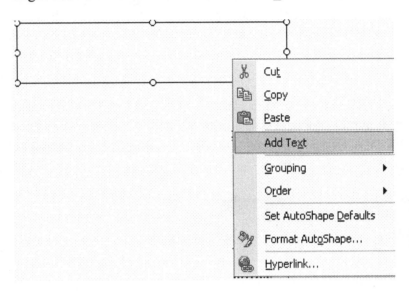

Type in the required text in bold
(by clicking **B** in the formatting toolbar).
Leave the first line blank and center align the text
(by clicking ≡ in the formatting toolbar).

INTRODUCTORY LEVEL JAVASCRIPT

Change the font color of the text to yellow by highlighting the text and then clicking on the small arrow next to the **A** ▾ icon in the Formatting toolbar. You should now see the following drop down. From this, select the yellow color.

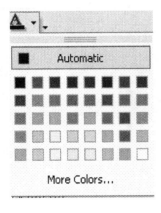

The highlighted text in the text box should now become yellow in color (once you unselect it, of course).

Please note that as stated in the introduction, at the time when the book was sent to the publisher, the intention was to publish the entire book in color. However due to certain logistics that arose in the last minute, the book interior had to be published in black and white. Thus for the reader's convenience, I have uploaded the pages where color is important on the following website:

http://www.wbook.info

Readers can go to the above website and download the relevant sections in color.

Your text box should now look as follows:

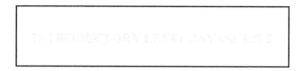

As you can see, the text is practically invisible. Therefore, we must now change the background color. Right click on the text box and select Format AutoShape…

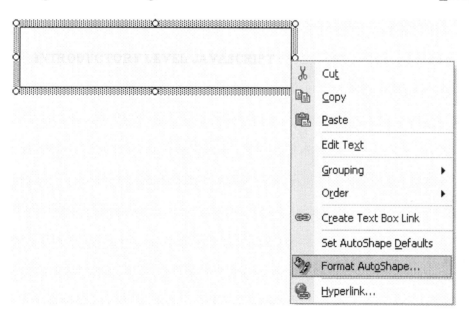

You should now see the following screen.

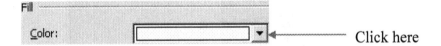

These are the different options for the text box. In order to change the background color for the text box, you must click on the small arrow next to the color field under Fill

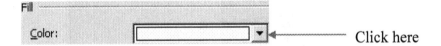

You should now see the following drop-down.

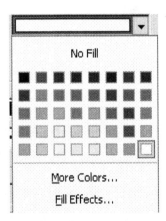

Select Blue from this menu. The area before the small arrow should now be colored blue.

Click on the small arrow again and select Fill Effects...

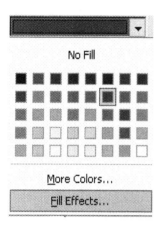

You will now see the following screen.

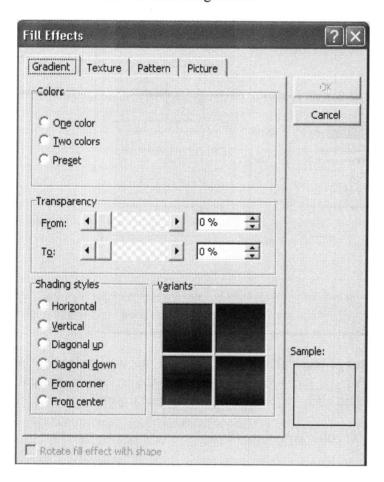

From the Variants select the one which has the dark blue shading in the middle (i.e. the second one in the first column).

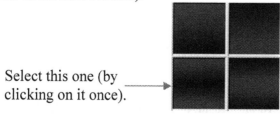

Select this one (by clicking on it once).

Now click on OK. You will now see the Format AutoShape dialog box, click OK again.
Your text box should now look as follows.

Right-click on the text box again and select Format AutoShape.

You should now see the following screen.

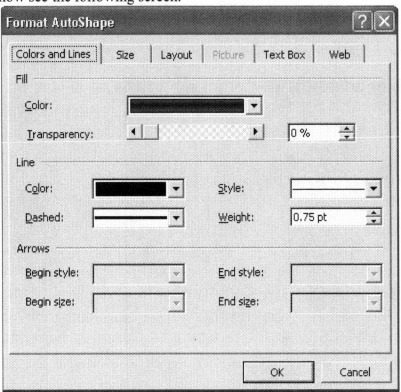

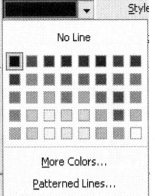 The settings under the heading Line are for the borders of the text box, you can see that there is a Color: option present. Once again click on the small arrow beside Color:

Select the color Turquoise ( ).

The area before the small arrow should now be colored turquoise

On the right of the color option, there should also be a Style option, click on the small arrow next to the line following Style

You should now see a number of lines drop-down. Click on the line that says 2 to the left of it. Now click on OK and you will again see the Format AutoShape dialog box; click on OK once again.

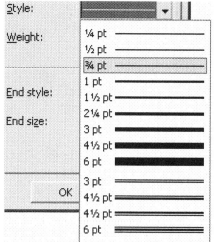

Your title is now complete and should look as follows:

INTRODUCTORY LEVEL JAVASCRIPT

The following pages show different titles which have all been made using Microsoft Word. These titles can be made easily by playing around with the options in the Format AutoShape dialog box.

Please note that as stated in the introduction, at the time when the book was sent to the publisher, the intention was to publish the entire book in color. However due to certain logistics that arose in the last minute, the book interior had to be published in black and white. Thus for the reader's convenience, I have uploaded the pages where color is important on the following website:

http://www.wbook.info

Readers can go to the above website and download the relevant sections in color.

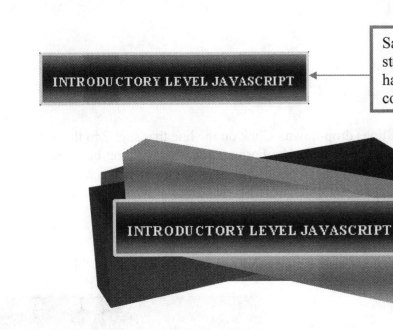

INTRODUCTORY LEVEL JAVASCRIPT

Same method as for the step by step example except the text box has a different background color.

The way to make t background 3D rectangles is creating three text boxes, addi color and making them 3 using the 3-D Style icon in t Drawing toolbar ( ). Y must click on the small arr and select the appropriate shap

INTRODUCTORY LEVEL JAVASCRIPT

Same method as for the step by step example except the text box has a light yellow background with blue text. The shading for the background is the bottom right one under the heading Variants in the Fill Effects dialog box.

Try to figure out the next four designs yourself. HINT: You can place a text box inside another text box.

INTRODUCTORY LEVEL JAVASCRIPT

INTRODUCTORY LEVEL JAVASCRIPT

INTRODUCTORY LEVEL JAVASCRIPT

INTRODUCTORY LEVEL JAVASCRI

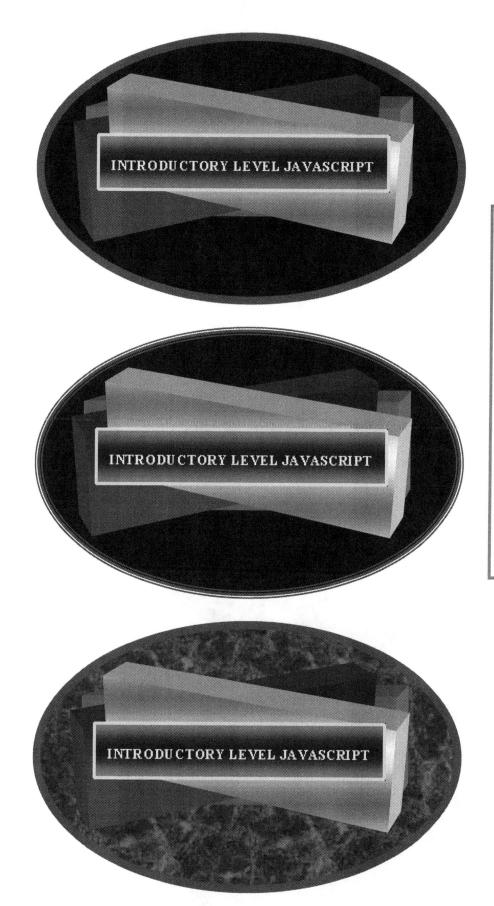

All the logos that follow have been made using the same basic method. The technique of making the inside of the ellipse is shown on the previous page. To achieve the different effects, the borders of the ellipse have been changed and a background texture has been used instead of having a colored background in some cases. Just play around with the text box settings to achieve different effects.

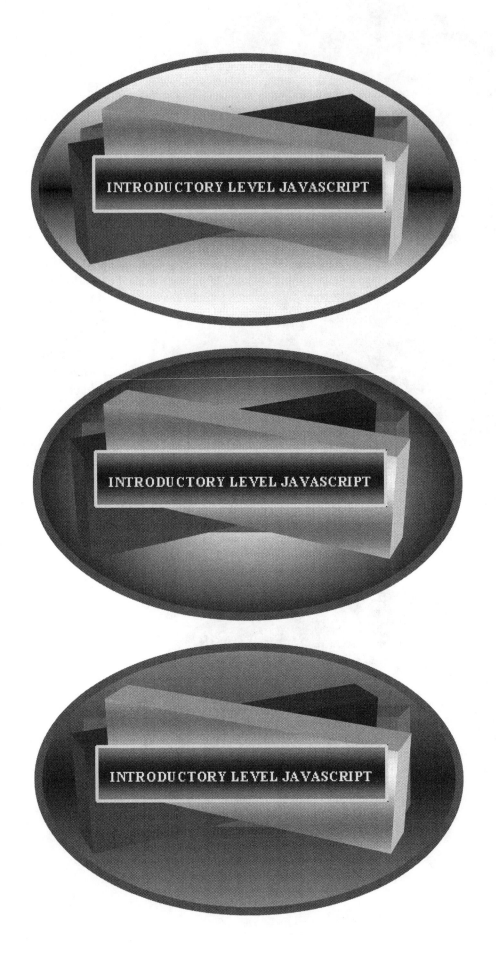

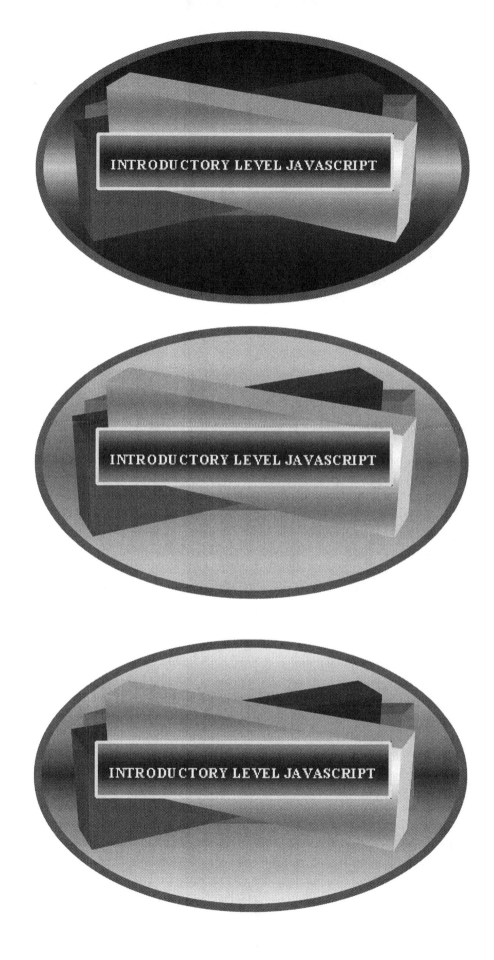

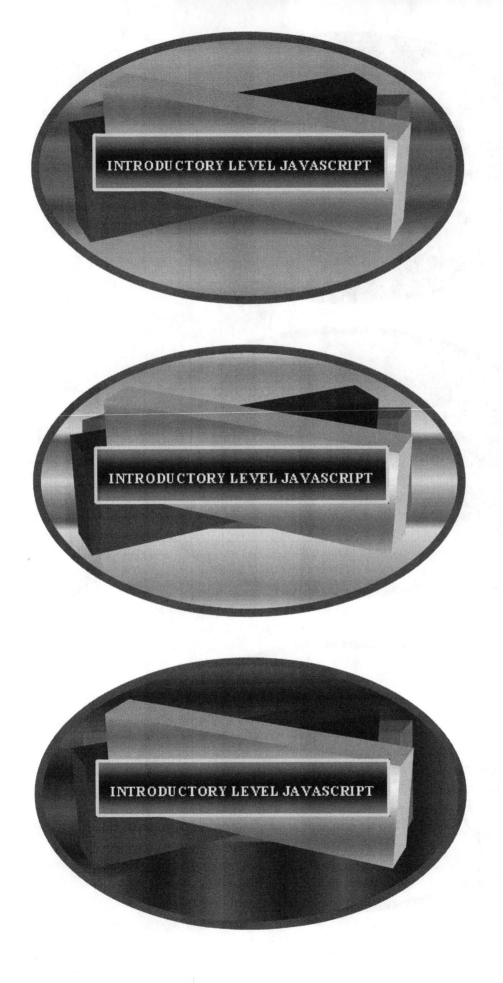

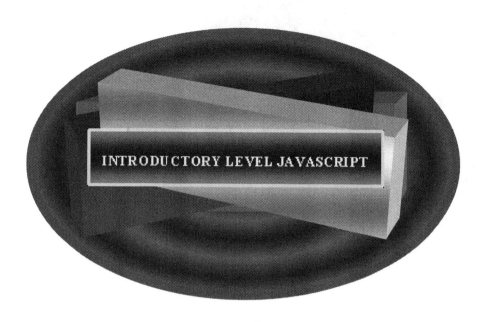

INTRODUCTORY LEVEL JAVASCRIPT

INTRODUCTORY LEVEL JAVASCRIPT

Background texture is not from Microsoft Word in this case

INTRODUCTORY LEVEL JAVASCRIPT

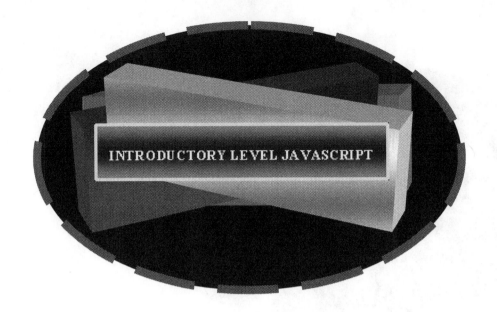

Try to figure out how the following title has been created. (Clue: There are two text boxes being used).

The following are some questions and answers which I strongly recommend you read. The answers might be a bit long but that is due to the fact that I have tried to include as much relevant information as possible.

Can I make a living off HTML?

This is a very frequently asked question. To put it simply, there is not much hope of finding a job as a web master if you **only** know HTML. When HTML was designed, it was not made to control the layout. The use of HTML stand-alone is a bit limited. In order for one to be an effective web designer, one needs to learn other tools in addition to HTML to be effective.

CSS (Cascading Style Sheets), however, gives a bit more control over what your page looks like but it is still not enough to be employed as a webmaster. For this reason, in order to be a paid web designer, you usually need to know ASP or Perl or some other programming languages. You would also need to be comfortable with programs and languages such as Flash and Javascript. There are no set requirements but the more you know, the better the chance you stand at finding a job in this ever growing field.

One way you could try finding a job is by setting up a website and on it you could say that for a simple HTML page, "$x" is the cost per hour for making the page. You could also post your resume or CV on specific websites.

To be quite frank, most of the websites you will see are not that fancy and you could more or less recreate them without facing many problems. Making a website too complicated may not always be the best option; you should also consider the type of people (traffic) you expect to visit the site. If the layout is too hard to understand for a novice, he will probably not waste any time trying to figure it out and most likely will just close the site.

What is CSS?

CSS is actually part of the HTML 4.0 specification. However, it was not covered in this book as it is thought to be somewhat advanced and this book is primarily aimed at beginners (and as a reference guide for more advanced users). CSS stands for Cascading Style Sheets. It can be quite useful as it allows you to separate the actual content of your webpage from its style. This can make it easier for you to update your webpage. For example, if you decided to change the font type of your webpage to "Black Chancery" from "Times New Roman", you would have to change the type in all the <font> tags in the source code. With CSS, you can define the fonts of your webpage in a separate file and if you wish to change the font, you would merely have to change it once in the CSS file. This is only one of the uses of CSS. The disadvantage of CSS is that it is not compatible with some older browsers and is also not completely compatible with somewhat newer ones. Despite this, your next step after finishing this book should be to learn CSS as it is a very useful technology. Some of the tags that have been used in this book have actually been deprecated. This does not mean that these tags can no longer be used. It merely means that these tags are not recommended for use by the W3C (World Wide Web Consortium – develops technologies and protocols for the web. See http://www.w3.org/ for more information). The reason for the deprecation in a lot of the cases was merely to encourage people to make use of CSS for style instead of HTML. Note that learning CSS will allow you to work more easily with the style of your webpage and is a recommendation of the W3C. You will not have to unlearn anything you have been taught in this book in order to learn CSS, you will merely have to add to your knowledge. The main reason I decided not to cover it in depth here is that although it is useful, it seems quite intimidating at first and is enough to discourage the novice web designer. The natural progression is to first become adequately acquainted with HTML which I have aimed to do in this book. I would recommend that you use an online tutorial to learn CSS. The basics may seem like a lot to remember at first but essentially it encompasses using the same principle applied throughout the language.

More about CSS

Cascading style sheets can be used in an HTML document in three ways:

1. **Inline style sheet:** The style elements are added directly to the HTML tag.
2. **Internal style sheet:** The style elements are included in the head section of the HTML document.
3. **External style sheet:** The style elements are saved in a separate file (CSS file). This is useful and popular because it separates the actual content of the webpage from the presentational layout.

Why would you use inline style sheets?

Inline style sheets defeat one of the main uses of CSS. Using CSS allows you to specify the formatting of a specific element which is then automatically used for all the elements of the same type; for example, you may specify all the paragraphs to be right aligned. However, if you want one of the paragraphs to be centered, you should use inline style sheets in this case. Therefore, inline style sheets are used when you want to override a specific external command on an internal style sheet tag.

Say that you specified the font color of the webpage text to be "white" in an external style sheet and had also specified the font color as "yellow" in an internal style sheet and as "green" in an inline style sheet. The font color for the text in the webpage will be yellow with the exception of the text which is within the inline style sheet (which will be green). None of the text would be white in color as the external style sheet command was superseded by the internal style sheet.

What is the next step after reading this book?

After you finish with this book, you should attempt to learn more about Cascading Style Sheets as they are in quite extensive use nowadays. You should also read some other HTML tutorials which are meant for advanced level HTML users. The reason for this is there are numerous tags that HTML utilizes and more advanced books would be able to shed light on less frequently used tags that I may not have mentioned. (Be sure to be on the lookout for other more advanced books to be written by me at some point too!)

After that you should concentrate on learning some more advanced JavaScript. If you are really serious about being a webmaster, then you should learn DHTML along with C, Perl, ASP or Flash after you are done with Javascript.

NOTE: There are many online resources available for learning programming and web-designing languages. However, you should ensure that you choose well-reputed sites as there is no guarantee of the validity of information found on many websites.

What is DHTML?

DHTML is short for Dynamic HyperText Markup Language. It is **NOT** another name for HTML. It is neither a computer language. It is more or less a name given to a way of enhancing a web page.

Don't get confused: If you see the words Dynamic HyperText Markup Language for the first time, you might just think that it is html and the word dynamic has just been added to make it look fancy. However, this is **completely** incorrect. When one starts out, do not get baffled by the fact that when you look at DHTML tutorials, for example, and you do not come across any of the tags/concepts in other html tutorials.

What is XHTML?

XHTML (eXtensible HyperText Markup Language) is said to be the next generation of web designing. It should be very easy for you to learn XHTML now that you know HTML. XHTML is basically just HTML with a few distinctions. XHTML at its most basic level just merely adds on a few rules. For example: The HTML tags **must** be in lower-case. XHTML is also case-sensitive and the order of the tags must be retained.

If you know HTML, it should probably take you an hour or so to grasp onto the concepts of XHTML.

How do I make an animation; how do I get it on my site?

Most of you will have come across the word '**animation**' while browsing the net or when reading an article. I would expect that a majority of you will know what it means but to save the rest of you the trouble of having to look it up in the dictionary, I will explain it to you. Animations are those moving pictures (or 'cartoons') that you see on websites.

Basically an animation is merely a series of pictures which are displayed in a certain sequence such that it gives rise to the overall effect of making the pictures appear to be in motion.

So how do you make an animation? Well, you need programs for making animations. There is a wide-range of programs available to choose from. Some programs already have tailor-made animations in them that you can use as is or edit them as you see fit.

Getting an animation onto your website is very simple. The steps are given below:

1) Save the animation in GIF format.
2) Insert the following line into the source code (where appropriate). <a href = "animation name.**gif**">This is an animation </a>
3) Save the file and view the page.

As you can see, it is exactly the same method as used for inserting an image. The **only** difference is that the **extension** of the file is '.gif'

NOTE: If you want to make simple animations, such as a picture moving across the screen, I recommend you learn DHTML as it can be used to make short animations.

Can you insert page break using HTML?

There is no way of inserting a page break using html. Page breaks depend on the font size, type, etc. HTML was designed to be a device-independent language. Obviously, when a person prints your page, it will get printed on as many pages as needed.

Word of advice: When you learn programming languages or web designing related languages, make sure that the language that you are using is well-renowned. The reason for this is that if you are using some unheard of language, chances are that the popular browsers will not support it which means that it won't work on all browsers. If a language is not popular, that can be an indication that it is not very useful.

Is HTML a programming language?

HTML is **NOT** a programming language. The reason for this is that you can not use HTML to make programs. So what is HTML then? HTML is a **markup** language.

Who invented HTML?

HTML is a subset of another more general language, SGML (Standard Generalized Markup Language). Tim Berners-Lee of the Massachusetts Institute of Technology (MIT) invented HTML while working at the European Organization for Nuclear Research (CERN). He is also the inventor of the World Wide Web.

Are programming languages similar to HTML?

No, programming languages are quite different than HTML. There are quite a few concepts to understand, such as variables, etc., whereas in HTML you merely need to understand the basic syntax and you could simply learn the tags. HTML, in my opinion, is one of the easiest computer languages to learn. Programming languages tend to be harder to master especially since there are many concepts to grasp onto. If you want to step into the world of programming and are a newbie, I suggest you start off with BASIC. BASIC is quite simple. BASIC cannot be used to make large programs such as Microsoft Word. However, it will at least help give an overview of the concepts of programming. I believe that the easiest programming language is LOGO. LOGO may be easy but it is primarily aimed at children (to teach them the fundamentals of programming). If you want to learn more extensively used languages, I suggest you try out C++ or Visual Basic.

NOTE: The reason that there are so many programming languages is that some are more popular for certain applications than others. Some are good for business management while others are better for scientific programs and so on. I recommend you always look up the main purpose of the language before you actually start learning it. For example, if you don't have the resources to set up a computer network, it wouldn't be of much use if you started reading the tutorial of a network programming language to use at home (unless you had access to such a network at an educational institution).

I have frequently seen % signs followed by numbers in URLs. What are these characters used for?

URLs must be written in US-ASCII character set. Basically, if you want to use characters that are not part of this set, they have to be encoded. The method for encoding these characters is quite simple. All you have to do is replace the required character with a percent sign that is followed by two hexadecimal numbers. The value of the hexadecimal numbers corresponds to the position of the character in the ASCII character set. Examples of encoded characters are %3B and %2F which denote semicolon and slash respectively.

Which part of the URL is the domain?

The word domain is used quite generally and it can get confusing as to what it actually refers to. There are different classes of domains. The right most part of the URL is referred to as the **top-level domain** or **TLD** for short. The second right most part of the URL (before the period) is called the **second-level domain**. The third right most part of the URL is called the **third-level domain** and so on.

For example: www.mywebsite.com

The above website has the following domains.

com → is the "top-level domain"
mywebsite → is the "second-level domain"
www → is the "third-level domain"

NOTE: Domains that represent specific countries such as .uk are also called Country Code Top-Level Domains (ccTLD).

Why are there so many different (top-level) domain names?

Each domain name is for a specific type of organization. Below is a list of some of the more popular domain names along with what entity they represent.

.com → Commercial entities
.net → Network providers
.org → Organization
.gov → Government entities
.edu → Educational institutes (primarily of the US)

Is it possible for me to start my own top-level domain name?

The Internet **SOC**iety (ISOC) controls the Internet's infrastructure. You can not start your own top-level domain name.

In 2002, ISOC decided that the domains were too overcrowded and therefore, was planned on creating new domains. However, in order to submit an idea for a new domain, an application fee of fifty thousand dollars was set. Furthermore, organizations also had to prove to ISOC that the domain would serve a specific purpose and final approval was up to ICANN (Internet Corporation For Assigned Names and Numbers, which is another important body that is responsible for certain aspects of the Internet).

There is an alternative method of setting up your own top-level domain but it is quite useless. There are some companies that allow you to set-up your own top-level domain. However, there is a catch. The websites which will have these special top-level domains will require the users to have special software in order to view them. Hence, the general public will be unable to view the website unless they have the software installed. If you find a website claiming that you can have the top level domain of your choice, beware that the website will only be accessible to certain people which have the program installed. Therefore, your best option is to register a website which uses one of the already available top-level domains so that your website is not limited to a certain audience.

You will have noted that this book not only teaches you HTML but also serves as your guide to what your next steps should be. This book was written while keeping in mind the average user who has no programming experience and is starting out his excursion to becoming a computer expert.

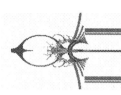 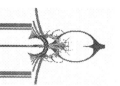

Hacking and cracking are the two topics that this final chapter will cover. These are ethically controversial issues which I believe that the reader needs to be aware of. For this reason, I decided to include some information on hacking and cracking so that you have a general idea of what they encompass.

Hacking

Hacking is the art of breaking into computer systems. This ranges from hacking into email accounts to hacking into computer systems. Hacking is ILLEGAL unless you take permission, in advance, from the owner of the computer system (that you are about to hack).

Most users will have at one time or another tried to find out the secrets behind hacking although many will have been unsuccessful in their attempts. The reason being that hacking can get a bit complicated depending on the methods you choose to accomplish it.

This section will merely scrape the surface of hacking and will not give you instructions on how to hack into computer systems or email accounts.

Hacking is commonly undertaken by exceptional computer experts who are usually programmers. Hackers sometimes hack into security systems for companies merely to warn them of the flaws in their system so that they can better safeguard themselves from destructive hackers. Hackers have their own language, which is called "1337", pronounced as "leet". Not all hackers have the same habits though. There are different classes of hackers and each one has their own style.

Hackers don't usually use their real names, they instead use nicknames referred to as their "handle". A common handle for a hacker would, for example, look something like "K-rad the 1337 hax0r".

Hackers sometimes hack to see if they can overcome the security systems of major companies; they see it as a challenge rather then do it with criminal intent. However, they sometimes end up unintentionally costing companies large sums of money.

Hackers are disliked by many people and are said to be criminals. Hackers claim their innocence usually by saying they are just merely curious and want to learn more about systems.

Hacking is done in a number of ways. Some of the ways hacking is done are listed below:

1) Using programming languages.
2) Telnet
3) Using Trojan horses like Sub 7
4) Key loggers

A Trojan horse is a program which claims to be something useful and is in fact malicious code. Trojan horses don't replicate themselves unlike viruses and worms. There are some Trojan horses that are for hacking purposes. For example, a Trojan horse that looks for AOL passwords and sends it back to the hacker. There are also Trojan horses which allow hackers to gain remote control of your system.

Make sure you have anti-trojan software installed on your computer; don't rely solely on your anti-virus software.

Key loggers are a method of hacking whereby the hacker installs a program called a key logger onto the system. This program records everything that is typed by the user. When the user types his password, this too is recorded. This is then sometimes automatically emailed to the hacker or else the hacker has to retrieve the log files on the machine.

There is one method of hacking which neither requires a computer or any technical knowledge, it merely depends on the gullibility of the company employees and your social skills. "Social Engineering" is the term used for such hacking. An example of this is as follows. Suppose there is a naïve secretary in the company and you want her password so you call her up claiming that you work in the company and that there has been a problem with her account so some data was lost. Then you tell her that you need to have her password in order to look into the problem. Taking advantage of naivety of people can be a form of hacking!

UNIX is perhaps the most commonly used operating system used to hack as it is well adapted to this purpose.

Cracking

Cracking is perhaps not as popular as hacking but it also requires hard work to learn. So what is cracking? Software developers make programs and release demo versions of their software, which have restrictions on them such as the demo will expire after 30 days or you can not save files, etc. In most cases, you purchase the software and you will be provided a serial number which you have to enter in the program and all the restrictions will be removed. Using cracking, you can register the product without having to buy it. This is done by going into the source code of the program and looking for the method used by the program to work out whether the serial entered is correct and in turn you work out the serial number of the software package (without buying it). Note that there are different methods of protecting software packages such as using programs like Soft Lock. I will not always be just a matter of finding the validation rule for the serial number.

People who crack programs need some software and also knowledge of **Assembly languages**. There are, however, extensive websites available on the net which provide them with cracks for programs. There are different types of cracks. With some of them, it is only a matter of opening the file and copying the serial number and pasting it into the program that it is for. There also exist patches for programs which are applied to the program's exe file. Note that cracks are just about always distributed as zip files. Instructions normally accompany the crack.

WARNING: Hacking is illegal unless you obtain the permission of the concerned party in advance. Cracking software packages is also illegal.

There are a lot of viruses on the net which claim to be hacking tools. Especially in peer-2-peer networks, like Kazaa, you are bound to come across a virus when searching for hacking tools.